# CHINESE VEGETABLE AND VEGETARIAN COOKING

Kenneth Lo first came to London at the age of six, when his father was appointed consul to the Chinese Embassy. Now in his eighties, he and his English wife Anne run the highly successful restaurant Memories of China in Chelsea Harbour, where their cookery school is also based. In his long and varied career he has been a diplomat, lecturer, journalist, radio and television celebrity, and professional tennis player. He has combined being a restaurateur with his many other interests for the past twenty-five years. He is author of several successful books on Chinese cooking and has recently published his autobiography.

# Chinese Vegetable and Vegetarian Cooking

## KENNETH LO

*faber and faber*

LONDON · BOSTON

First published in 1974
by Faber and Faber Limited
3 Queen Square London WC1N 3AU
This revised paperback edition published in 1995

Phototypeset by Intype, London
Printed in England by Clays Ltd, St Ives plc

A CIP record for this book is
available from the British Library

ISBN 0–571–10652–8

2 4 6 8 10 9 7 5 3 1

# Contents

# Foreword

The impact of Chinese cooking on Western cuisine seems to have had only a minimal influence during all the centuries gone by. In the main the West was not aware that the Chinese have been using stir-frying as one of their most frequently employed cooking methods for nearly two millennia and up until the mid-seventies, when this book was first published, the wok was practically unknown in Western kitchens.

Since those days, there has been a huge increase in the number of vegetarians and much greater interest is taken in vegetable cookery as an art in itself, whether for vegetarians or otherwise. People in general have become far more health-conscious and one of the aims of this book is to help restore the very important balance between meat and vegetable which the human body requires, something I have been urging for over a decade.

# Introduction

Cooking and serving a Chinese meal, vegetarian or otherwise, presents somewhat different problems from cooking and serving a Western one, since a Chinese meal is usually communal. It is rather like a buffet, generally hot, consisting of a fair number of dishes, or it is a banquet, involving a dozen or more courses. The major task is therefore to produce a number of dishes to serve at the same time, as at home, or a series of dishes which must be served one after another (as during a party meal or banquet). Unlike the task of producing soup or starter, main course and dessert for a Western meal, a Chinese meal involves a much greater number of dishes: 4–6 for a home meal, and 12–15 upwards for a banquet. The display element involved makes Chinese vegetable cooking a veritable 'garden of dishes', almost a 'flower show' in its visual appeal. The great profusion of colours is possible partly because by the Chinese method vegetables are never overcooked, which kills the freshness and colour, but are treated like a series of 'hot salads'. Vegetables can be presented singly, cooked with an eye to purity, or assembled together, often after a minimal amount of cooking, or prepared by different methods with the aim of achieving the most interesting orchestration of colour, texture and flavour.

The variety in texture in Chinese cooking often derives from the different methods of cooking different ingredients: deep-fried foods are crispy; stewed or simmered foods are tender and saucy; while quick-fried foods are fresh and crunchy. Variety and balance come from the careful blending of flavours resulting from the choice of materials and the superimposition of one type of flavour upon another: such as dried or salted foods on fresh foods, or meat on vegetables; or through the common practice of impregnating hot oil with the flavours of strong vegetables (ginger, garlic, onion) which in turn are used to cook and flavour the main component of the dish. The flavouring agents – such as wine, tofu cheese, soya sauce, hoisin sauce, meat broths, sugar, etc. – are usually introduced only during the concluding stages of the cooking.

When we embarked on this book it occurred to both my publisher and myself that one of the best ways of organizing the material was to divide and group it under the different methods of cooking, and then to subdivide it further into the different vegetables employed, or into the different main groups of dishes being produced (soups, salads, desserts, pastas, etc.). An arrangement of this kind should be a great help in encouraging the reader to tackle Chinese cooking. By having each chapter concentrating on one method of cooking, the book should make it much easier for the average Westerner to conduct an initial 'run in', after which some of the mystique still surrounding Chinese cooking will have evaporated. After all, one of the purposes of this book, apart from introducing Chinese vegetable and vegetarian cooking, is to help in dispelling some of the mystery which still pervades any subject connected with the Chinese.

With Chinese cooking, as with any other, the principal factors involved are cutting, flavouring and heating. Once these are mastered, everything falls into place, and after that all this is necessary is some experience and increasing acquaintance, both in cooking and eating, for success to be assured. But because of the Chinese practice of marrying one type of food with another, and superimposing one type of flavouring or method of cooking on to another, the number of dishes which can be concocted is mainly a question of permutation, which means that the repertoire at the cook's command is almost limitless. One of the fascinations of Chinese cooking, vegetable or otherwise, is that in learning new ways of cutting, flavouring and heating, you obtain the key to a whole new culinary world – one which has given unfailing pleasure to countless millions and generations of Chinese in an otherwise often drab existence. Fortunately the appeal of good food is international, so if you can master Chinese cooking, as many Westerners I know seem to have done, you can be assured of being able to gratify yourself and a great many other people – no matter where in the world you live.

One other point should be elaborated before I conclude this Introduction: although there is a definite distinction, just as in Western cooking, between a vegetarian and a non-vegetarian dish, in Chinese cooking the distinction between a meat and a vegetable dish is only a matter of degree. Thus, a Chinese dish is a vegetable one where a vegetable is the main constituent (usually over three-quarters of the weight), and a meat one where meat provides the predominant character (over one-quarter of the ingredients). Since both vegetable and meat are present in the bulk of Chinese dishes, this is probably the area where by far the largest number of Chinese dishes are produced. For this reason, if for no other, it is an important part of Chinese cuisine, and in a book like this, which is meant to be practical, such dishes should be represented. I have therefore, for every applicable series of vegetarian dishes, indicated a corresponding parallel series of non-vegetarian ones. Since in the majority of cases the methods of cooking employed are almost exactly the same – the difference being only a matter of flavouring, or the addition of some shredded or thinly sliced meat at some point in the process – the suggestion or addition of a few key ingredients should make each situation or process amply clear. However, as the book is centred around vegetables, all the non-vegetarian dishes included are still predominantly vegetable in character.

Since this book is designed for use in the average Western kitchen – vegetarian or otherwise – its aims are purely practical. It offers no apology, therefore, for making fairly free use of such foods as dairy produce (milk, cream, cheese, etc.) which are not often employed in Chinese cookery, except in frontier regions, but certainly can sometimes be used to advantage. There are other concessions to the modern kitchen, where modern equipment, such as the electric blender, pressure-cooker, thermostatically-controlled oven, and even the can-opener, can sometimes help to reduce originally difficult or laborious operations to comparative simplicity.

Times change, and so can Chinese cooking.

As I have already said, one of the principal appeals of Chinese vegetable cooking lies in the fascination of combining and presenting a whole array of dishes, a profusion of taste, shape, colour and texture, and thereby creating a veritable 'garden' on the dining table. Such a seductive spread, particularly appealing to the garden-conscious British, might even tempt some of you to greater efforts in the garden. With the prospect of such a delicious reward for their efforts, many gardeners might well dig with greater heart to produce the vegetable dishes which they will enjoy and which will be acclaimed by all who share them. What can contribute more to domestic bliss, or to edifying and civilizing society?

## CUTTING, COOKING (HEATING), AND FLAVOURING

Cutting, heating and flavouring are the three basic processes in cooking or preparing food. At first glance it seems that they could hardly differ very much from one type of cooking to another. After all, the possibility of variation must be limited: there are only so many ways of cutting, heating or flavouring food. But when observed and considered in detail, the possibility of finesse in each of the processes is considerable, and when one form of finesse is combined with another, the variety of end-products which can be produced is impressive. It is the exploitation of the finesse possible in each of these basic processes and the combination of them that makes Chinese cooking so wide-ranging and distinctive. Yet we must not allow this 'wheels within wheels' concept of Chinese cooking to develop into a mystique which may cloud the fact that Chinese cooking is basically quite simple, and that Chinese vegetable and vegetarian cooking are even simpler, for they are only a part of the larger whole. Incongruous though it sounds, Chinese cooking can be compared with riding a bicycle. Once you can mount a bicycle and stay on it, you can almost do anything with it, without fully understanding the complex relation of forces between one wheel and another; so too with Chinese cooking.

Since neither in cooking nor in bicycling are we trying to probe the truth of the universe, we must come down quickly to essentials, and the 'brass-tacks' of Chinese cooking techniques are:

## Cutting

In Chinese cooking, cutting takes two things into consideration: the type of heat being used and the shape of the principal substance to be cooked. If this latter is lengthy or elongated, e.g. noodles, the supplementary materials are cut in more or less the same elongated shape. If the principal substance is square or round, such as peas, the other materials are also chopped or diced into small pieces of more or less the same size. If the food is to be cooked for a fair length of time (2–3 hours), all the cutting necessary is a little trimming, and if the supplementary materials are added at the outset, they too only require the minimal amount of cutting or trimming. If, however, they are added towards the end of the cooking, or when the main substance is already cooked, then they will have to be reduced to a much smaller size – or even minced –

before they are added. Chopped or minced chives or spring onion are sprinkled over numerous Chinese dishes before serving.

Since a great many Chinese dishes are cooked rapidly by stir-frying, to facilitate heating through (for seconds, or only a minute or two), foods cooked in this way are usually shredded, sliced into very thin slices, or chopped into small cubes the size of a sugar-lump or half that size. Leaf vegetables are cut into one- or two-inch size pieces; hard vegetables are often 'rolling-cut', i.e. cut diagonally or slantwise after each quarter turn, so that a large surface can be exposed to heating and flavouring. Large chunks of foods which have been cooked for a good length of time are often cut into bite-size pieces before serving, which are simpler to handle with chopsticks and easier to eat.

## Heating

Except for stir-frying, which is distinctive to Chinese cooking, the methods used in Chinese cooking are basically much the same as those used in Western cooking: boiling, stewing, deep-frying, shallow-frying, roasting, baking, steaming, grilling, barbecuing, smoking, etc., apart from one or two specialized forms of heat treatment, such as hot-burying (in salt, mud or sand), hot-splashing (with oil), dry-scorching (on dry metal plate or griddle), simmering in herbal broth (hot-marinading), or 'drunken-marinading' (which is in fact not a heat treatment, but a cold flavouring process used to complete a cooking process). But it is in the subdivision under each category, and in the use of one method in conjunction with another that Chinese cooking begins to exploit its potential. Below I give the gist of the methods commonly used, but they are described in greater detail later in the book in the appropriate places:

## BOILING

a) *Plunged-boiling:* thinly sliced material plunged into boiling water or broth for very short period of cooking and then taken out for immediate eating.
b) *Deep-boiling:* food boiled in quantities of water with no seasoning and dipped in piquant sauces when served.
c) *Long-simmering:* simmering over very low heat with or without much flavouring materials.

Foods prepared in these ways without flavouring materials are usually further cooked by quick deep-fry and then eaten with sauce, or sliced and further cooked for a short period in a small casserole with selected flavouring materials added.

## STEWING

a) *Red-cooking:* with soya sauce.
b) *White-cooking:* food is plain cooked in light-coloured broth (occasionally with milk, cream, or beaten egg white added).
c) *Hot-assembly:* a short form of stewing, where a number of foods and ingredients are cooked separately by different methods and then assembled together in a pot or casserole and further cooked together for a short period of time with the addition of a few selected flavouring ingredients.

## STEAMING

a) *Open steaming:* foods (often seasoned and marinaded) are subjected to a comparatively short (5–25 minutes) but intense period of steaming in an open dish.
b) *Closed steaming:* foods in a closed heatproof dish are subjected to long periods of steaming (an hour or two or more). This process is not unlike double-boiler cooking, and ensures an even temperature throughout the whole period of cooking.
c) *Terminal steaming:* steaming is used as a 'sealing' process by which foods already cooked by other methods, such as

stir-fry, braising, etc., are further tenderized and assembled together for a period of high-intensity steaming.

### DEEP-FRYING

a) *Plain deep-frying.*
b) *Battered deep-frying.*
c) *Short period deep-frying:* a preliminary or initial process for cooking by other methods: stir-frying, braising, hot-assembling. Such short deep-frying is to ordinary deep-frying as parboiling is to boiling.
d) *Deep-frying as a concluding process:* either after a period of steaming, long-simmering, or marinading.

### SHALLOW-FRYING

A process typical of shallow-frying is frying bread. In Chinese cooking, it is the usual method of crisping up one part of the food, usually the bottom, as in the case of Cantonese Fried Noodles, or Peking Pot-Stuck 'Raviolis' or wraplings, where foods which have been cooked in other ways – steaming or stir-frying – are crisped up by a period of shallow-frying, which also ensures that the dish is cooked through. If there is a shortage of oil, shallow-frying can do the work of deep-frying if the food is simply turned around in the hot oil in the pan.

### ROASTING AND BAKING

Roasting and baking are not often used for vegetable cooking in China, partly because few Chinese kitchens are equipped with an oven, and where there is one, it is usually reserved for cooking fowls or meat. But as every properly equipped Western kitchen has an oven, it can be easily adapted for Chinese cooking by using a casserole for:

a) Pot-roasting.
b) Hot-assembly (in a casserole).
c) Baking (wrapped in aluminium foil).
d) Slow open roasting (for such items as sweet potato).

e) Baking as a drying and crisping process – after braising or stewing.

## GRILLING AND BARBECUING

Grilling and barbecuing are again processes which are usually associated with meat cooking. In vegetable cooking they can usually be used in place of scorch-frying, where a slightly burnt taste is required, or dry-frying, where a drying-up, reducing process can be speeded up before the final stir-fry.

## SMOKING

Smoking is seldom used in cooking vegetables. Usually when a smoky flavour is part of a vegetable dish, it is achieved by introducing smoked meat or other materials during cooking.

## STIR-FRYING

Stir-frying is probably the most widely used method of cooking in China. It can be divided into several subdivisions or combined with a few other processes:

a) Quick stir-frying (plain).
b) Dry stir-frying (Kan Shao).
c) Wet stir-frying (Liao).
d) Stir-frying and braising.
e) Stir-frying and steaming.
f) Stir-frying and hot-assembly.
g) Stir-frying and scorch-frying.

## HOT AND COLD 'TOSSING'

'Tossing' (or Pan) is the process of tossing, as in salad-making, food, e.g. raw or parboiled vegetable or cooked noodles, in hot or cold dressings and sauces (mostly hot).

## HOT-MARINADING (OR SIMMERING) IN HERBAL MASTER SAUCE (OR LOU)

It is a common practice in Chinese cooking to prepare a strong herbal broth with a soya sauce base in which foods are immersed and simmered for varying periods of time, until cooked. Food so prepared is often cooked for a further short period – by stir-fry, deep-fry or steaming – before being served. The subtlety of the flavour is varied by slightly varying the contents of the herbal Master Sauce, and by using other flavourers in the final cooking.

## *The Flavourers*

In Chinese food preparation flavourings are used in three stages:

a) *Before cooking:* as marinades.

b) *During the process of cooking:* sauces and seasonings.

c) *On the table:* as table condiments in the form of dips and mixes.

Flavourers come in several forms; these are some of the principal categories:

a) *Basic seasonings:* salt, pepper, sugar, vinegar, chilli, curry, five-spice powder, mustard, sesame oil (aromatic).

b) *Strong vegetables:* onion, spring onion, ginger, garlic.

c) *Soya bean products:* soya sauce, black beans (salted), soya paste (yellow and black), tofu (bean-curd) cheese, tofu cakes.

d) *Other sauces:* hoisin sauce, plum sauce, chilli sauce, tomato sauce, and two non-vegetarian sauces – shrimp sauce and oyster sauce.

e) *Dried, pickled, and salted vegetables:* dried mushrooms, salted cabbage, Chinese pickled greens (Red-in-Snow), hot-pickled Szechuan cabbage or ja choi (finely chopped gherkins are a good substitute), dried bamboo-shoots, dried lily bud stalks ('golden needles'), dried lotus root, dried tangerine peel, preserved turnip.

f) *Miscellaneous:* sesame paste (peanut butter can be used as a substitute), various wines.

In Chinese vegetable and vegetarian cooking quite a number of English or Western products are both convenient and useful: vegetable bouillon cube or powder, yeast extract or Marmite, and all the various pickles, chutneys, jams and preserves. I use sherry in quite a number of recipes: dry sherry is preferable. For non-vegetarians, a chicken stock cube can be conveniently used in the preparation of many dishes, for in Chinese cooking one of the most widely used non-vegetarian flavourers is concentrated chicken or meat broth, or 'meat gravy' (meat cooked with soya sauce).

This book is dedicated to all lovers of vegetables, including all vegetarians who enjoy their diet, but *not* to those who have taken to vegetables because they abhor meat and have to put up with them to exist. It is dedicated to all those who think that vegetables are one of God's gifts to man and as such should be thoroughly enjoyed and appreciated.

## NOTE ON VEGETABLE BROTH

Many of the recipes in this book call for Vegetable Broth. Ideally this should be the basic Chinese Vegetable Broth (see page 86); the Simplified Vegetable Broth (page 87), which takes less time to prepare, may also be used. Alternatively, dissolve 1 vegetable stock cube or 1 teaspoon of yeast extract or Marmite in $1^1/_2$ pints of hot water.

# METRIC MEASUREMENTS

Vegetables in the UK are still usually sold in pounds and ounces. For those more used to using metric measurements in cooking, approximate conversions are as follows:

| | | | |
|---|---|---|---|
| 1 oz | = 25 g | 9 oz | = 250 g |
| 2 oz | = 50 g | 10 oz | = 280 g |
| 3 oz | = 85 g | 11 oz | = 300 g |
| $1/_4$ lb | = 110 g | $3/_4$ lb | = 340 g |
| 5 oz | = 140 g | 13 oz | = 370 g |
| 6 oz | = 170 g | 14 oz | = 400 g |
| 7 oz | = 200 g | 15 oz | = 425 g |
| $1/_2$ lb | = 225 g | 1 lb | = 450 g |

$1/_2$ pint = 300 ml (nearly one third of a litre)
1 pint = 600 ml (just over half a litre)

# Quick Guide

Although eating Chinese has become familiar to people living in even quite small towns in Britain, cooking Chinese may still be thought of as something rather exotic. To enable the cook to start with the known, here is a list of the more common vegetables available in this country together with a selection of the recipes of which they form the main ingredient.

ASPARAGUS: Stir-braised Asparagus (p. 28); Deep-fried Marinaded Asparagus (p. 40); Hot-marinaded Asparagus Tips (p. 54); Clear-simmered Asparagus (p. 75); Asparagus and Bamboo-shoot Soup (p. 95).

AUBERGINE: Stir-braised Aubergine (p. 28); Quick Deep-fried Aubergine (p. 34); Deep-fried Marinaded Aubergine (p. 40); Hot-marinaded Aubergine (p. 54); Red-cooked Aubergines (p. 60).

BEANS, French: Plain Stir-fried Young Beans (p. 23); Stir-braised Beans (p. 27); Quick Deep-fried and Stir-fried French Beans (p. 37); Steamed French Beans in Hot Peanut Butter Sauce (p. 49); Hot-marinaded Stir-fried French Beans (p. 52); White-cooked French Beans (p. 67); French Beans Fu-Yung (p. 130); Bean-Curd Stir-fried with French Beans (p.140).

BEANS, Runner: Clear-simmered Runner Beans (p. 74).

BEAN SPROUTS: Plain Stir-fried Bean Sprouts (p. 20).

BROCCOLI: Stir-braised Broccoli (p. 26); Deep-fried Marinaded Broccoli (p. 40); Steamed Broccoli with Fu-Yung Sauce (p. 43); Red-cooked Broccoli (p. 61); White-cooked Broccoli (p. 67); Clear-simmered Broccoli (p. 74); Broccoli Soup (p. 96).

BRUSSELS SPROUTS: Stir-braised Brussels Sprouts (p. 27); Deep-fried Marinaded Brussels Sprouts (p. 40); Red-cooked Brussels Sprouts (p. 61); White-cooked Brussels Sprouts (p.67); Clear-simmered Brussels Sprouts (p. 74); Brussels Sprouts Soup (p. 96).

CABBAGE: Stir-braised Cabbage (p. 27); Quick Deep-fried Savoy (p. 35); Quick Deep-fried Sweet and Sour Savoy (p. 36); Steamed Cabbage and Spring Greens (p. 43); Hot-marinaded Cabbage with Sweet and Sour Sauce (p. 57); Red-cooked Cabbage (p. 62); White-cooked Cabbage (p. 65); Clear-simmered Cabbage (p. 74); Hot Cabbage Soup (p. 93); Heart of Cabbage Soup (p. 94); Cabbage and Celery Mustard Salad (p. 149).

CARROTS: Stir-braised Carrots (p. 28); Steamed Carrots and Parsnips in Hot Peanut Butter Sauce (p. 49); Hot-marinaded Carrots and Turnips (p. 53); Hot-marinaded Shredded Carrots (p. 58); Red-cooked Carrots (p. 63); Carrots, Cress and Cucumber Vegetable Rice (p. 107); Chinese Carrot Salad (p. 148).

CAULIFLOWER: Stir-braised Cauliflower (p. 26); Quick Deep-fried Cauliflower (p. 33); Deep-fried and Marinaded Cauliflower (p. 40); White-cooked Cauliflower (p. 66); Cauliflower Fu-Yung (p. 130).

CELERY: Plain Stir-fried Celery (p. 21); Quick Deep-fried Celery (p. 36); Hot-marinaded Celery (p. 53); Red-cooked Celery (p. 62); White-cooked Celery (p. 66); Clear-simmered Celery (p. 74); Celery Soup (p. 91); Cabbage and Celery Mustard Salad (p. 149).

COURGETTES: Stir-braised Courgettes (p. 28); Quick Deep-fried Courgettes (p. 34); White-cooked Courgettes (p. 67).

CUCUMBER: Strips of Cucumber Soup (p. 87).

LEEKS: Plain Stir-fried Young Leeks (p. 21); Leek Soup (p. 91).

LETTUCE: Plain Stir-fried Lettuce (p. 20); Quick-steamed Buttered Lettuce (p. 42); Lettuce Soup (p. 92); Clear-simmered Bean-Curd with Lettuce (p. 145).

MARROWS: Stir-braised Marrow (p. 28); Steamed Marrow Bowl

(p. 45); White-cooked Marrow (p. 67); Clear-simmered Marrow (p. 74).

MUSHROOMS: Quick Deep-fried Button Mushrooms (p. 38); Deep-fried Marinaded Mushrooms (p. 39); Mushroom Sauce (p. 82); Mushroom Soup (p. 90); Mushroom and Green Peas Vegetable Rice (p. 106).

ONION: Chinese Onion Soup (p. 97).

PARSNIPS: Steamed Parsnips and Carrots in Hot Peanut Butter Sauce (p. 49).

PEAS: Plain Stir-fried Green Peas (p. 25); Sweet Pea Soup (p. 100); Green Pea Soup (p. 101); Green Peas and Mushroom Vegetable Rice (p. 106).

POTATOES: Glazed Potato Chips (p. 166).

SPINACH: Plain Stir-fried Spinach (p. 18); Stir-fried Eggs with Spinach (p. 128); Bean-Curd Stir-fried with Spinach (p. 139); Spinach Soup (p. 88); Green Jade Soup (p. 89).

SPRING GREENS: Quick Deep-fried Cauliflower and Spring Greens (p. 33); Quick Deep-fried Spring Greens (p. 35); Steamed Spring Greens and Cabbage (p. 43); Heart of Spring Greens Soup (p. 94); Quick Deep-fried Sweet and Sour Spring Greens (p. 36).

TOMATOES: Plain Stir-fried Tomatoes (p. 22); Tomato Soup (p. 90).

TURNIPS: Hot-marinaded Turnips and Carrots (p. 53); Red-cooked Turnips (p. 63); Turnip Soup (p. 94).

WATERCRESS: Watercress Soup (p. 91).

# Stir-frying

Stir-frying consists of cooking foods which have been cut into thin slices, or into shreds, in a few tablespoons of peanut or sunflower oil (usually 2–3 tablespoons) in a frying-pan or wok over high heat, stirring and turning all the time. Because of the high heat, the food cooks rapidly and must be turned, scrambled and stirred continuously to prevent sticking and scorching. This method of cooking is also often termed 'quick-frying'. A more graphic and complete description of the process would be 'quick stir-frying'. The actual process usually starts by heating the oil in the middle of the pan and adding a small quantity of a few strongly flavoured vegetables such as onion, garlic and ginger (or any one of them); these are fried and stirred in the oil for a matter of a minute or less. This first stage impregnates the oil with the palate-stimulating flavour of these strong vegetables.

In the second stage the main ingredient, which has been shredded or sliced thin, is added to the flavour-impregnated oil. It is then turned in the hot oil for a minute or two, depending on the quantity; normally if this exceeds 1 lb, an extra minute or two may be required. If salt is sprinkled over the food at this stage, accompanied by vigorous stirring, the vegetables will often turn greener.

It is usually in the third stage that the flavourers are added: such as Vegetable Broth, soya sauce, soya paste, sugar, wine, vegetable bouillon powder, hoisin sauce, tomato sauce, chilli sauce, vinegar, mustard, sesame oil (for aroma), etc., or in the case of non-vegetarians such ingredients as concentrated chicken broth, meat gravy, shrimp sauce, etc. Adding these ingredients at this stage imparts more flavour to the food and also helps to prevent it from scorching. For foods and vegetables which do not require prolonged cooking, this is the final stage of the cooking. After a few more rapid turns and stirrings, the food can be put into a well-heated serving dish and served. The water has been released from the vegetable in its contact with the hot oil and hot metal of the pan and combines with the flavourers to produce ample sauce. The swift cooking makes for freshness and the ingredients retain much of their original food value.

Where more than one main ingredient is combined in the cooking, it is usual to add the one which requires longer cooking to the impregnated oil for a minute or two of stir-frying, then to push it to the sides of the pan and add a little more oil before adding the other ingredients to the middle of the pan. The second group of ingredients is stir-fried for a few minutes, then mixed with the first and combined with the flavourers in the general final stir-up. Quite often, even if a single type of vegetable is being cooked, the harder parts, such as the stalk, stem or root (thinly sliced), are put into the pan and cooked for an initial period before the tender leaves are added.

If great heat is used, as is often the case, some 'broth' might have to be added to the first ingredients to prevent scorching. With hard vegetables, such as asparagus, broccoli, carrots, turnips, string beans, potato, etc., parboiling may be advisable before stir-frying. In the case of the semi-hard vegetables, such as cabbage, celery, bamboo-shoots, cauliflower, spring greens, aubergines, courgettes, Brussels sprouts, etc., a short final period of braising is all that is required to tenderize them.

After the vegetables have been stir-fried, a little more liquid is added and a cover placed on the pan. The braising should be well-timed, and may last for 2–5 minutes, but the cover should be removed only once before the final stir-up and serving (lifting the cover frequently tends to make the vegetables turn yellow).

Simple quick stir-frying, without parboiling or braising, is ideal for soft vegetables or vegetables which require very little cooking. These include spinach, lettuce, bean sprouts, young leeks, watercress, young hearts of cabbage (Savoy), spring greens, tomatoes, sliced cucumber, garden peas, pea pods, etc.

For the foregoing variations in stir-frying, the best type of pan is a large deep-sided one fitted with a lid, both for short braising and to prevent splashing. The pan should not be heavy because for Chinese stir-fry cooking, heat should be conducted by the pan as swiftly as possible. A thick iron pan is also too heavy to be handled with dexterity. Since nowadays there is a good choice of equipment available, there should be no difficulty in obtaining just such a pan. With a pan like this on the cooker – gas is preferable to electricity – and all the usual seasonings in the kitchen cupboard – salt, pepper, vinegar, sugar, mustard, tomato purée – plus soya sauce, chilli sauce, Vegetable Broth and vegetable bouillon powder you should be ready to begin cooking Chinese vegetables or vegetarian dishes. If possible, you should also try to have at hand Chinese salted black beans, tofu cheese, hoisin sauce, sesame paste (or peanut butter), sesame oil and Chinese dried mushrooms (one of the most frequently used items in Chinese vegetable and vegetarian cooking).

For non-vegetarians, add concentrated chicken broth, made by adding chicken stock cube to chicken broth, shrimp sauce, oyster sauce, fish sauce and some red-cooked meat and gravy.

# QUICK STIR-FRIED DISHES

### Plain Stir-fried Spinach
(for 4–6 portions)

| | |
|---|---|
| 1¹/₂ lb spinach | 1¹/₂ tablespoons soya sauce |
| 3–4 tablespoons vegetable oil | 1 teaspoon sugar |

1 teaspoon salt
1 small onion
2 cloves garlic
2 slices ginger root
1 tablespoon sherry

$^{1}/_{2}$ teaspoon vegetable
  bouillon powder
$^{1}/_{2}$ tablespoon sesame oil
  (optional)

Remove the hard stems of the spinach, and then cut or tear the leaves into $1^{1}/_{2}$–2-inch squares. Chop and mince the onion. Crush garlic and shred ginger.

Heat the oil in a large frying-pan. Add onion, garlic and ginger. Stir-fry for 1 minute on a high heat. Add the spinach and sprinkle with salt. Spread the spinach over the pan. Turn and stir it in the oil until the vegetable is well coated (for about 2–3 minutes). Add sherry, soya sauce, vegetable bouillon powder and sugar. Continue to turn and stir more gently on a medium heat for another 2–3 minutes. Add sesame oil and turn the vegetable over once more. Serve on a very well-heated serving dish.

For non-vegetarians, the only difference will be to use $^{1}/_{2}$ a crushed chicken stock cube instead of vegetable bouillon powder during the second stage of the stir-frying and 1 tablespoon of melted lard or chicken fat at the final stage.

*Alternative Combinations*: Stir-fried Spinach can be combined with many other vegetables, but most often with mushrooms. Fresh mushrooms ($^{1}/_{4}$ lb) should be sliced in vertical halves and stir-fried for 2 minutes in $1^{1}/_{2}$ tablespoons of extra oil or butter and pushed to the sides of the pan before the spinach is added. Chinese dried mushrooms should be soaked and the stems discarded.

For non-vegetarians, $^{1}/_{4}$ lb of thinly sliced meat (beef, lamb, pork) is often used instead of mushrooms, especially when the meal contains no big meat dish. But connoisseurs, however, prefer the plain fried spinach.

## Plain Stir-fried Bean Sprouts

Bean sprouts can be stir-fried in precisely the same manner as the spinach in the previous recipe. For $1^1/_4$ lb of bean sprouts, use the same quantities of other ingredients; the cooking time too is much the same, although bean sprouts can be cooked for a slightly shorter period. One tablespoon of chopped chives or spring onion can be sprinkled over the dish before serving.

For *alternative combinations*, bean sprouts are most often combined with Chinese dried mushrooms or dried bamboo-shoots, which must be soaked and cut into shreds. About $^1/_6$–$^1/_4$ lb of these combines well with 1 lb of bean sprouts and an extra tablespoon of oil should be used for frying. If meat is combined with the bean sprouts, it too must be cut into thin shreds, and stir-fried for 2–3 minutes in an extra tablespoon of oil and $^1/_2$ teaspoon of salt before the bean sprouts are put into the pan. A couple of teaspoons of shrimp sauce or fish sauce greatly enhances the flavour.

Another vegetable which is often combined with bean sprouts is chilli pepper. This is usually shredded (the seeds are removed) and added to the oil with the garlic, onions, etc., for a short period of stir-frying before the bean sprouts are introduced. The result, Hot Plain Stir-fried Bean Sprouts, is a piquant dish.

## Plain Stir-fried Lettuce

Lettuce can be treated in precisely the same manner as spinach – Plain Stir-fried Spinach – except it requires even less cooking ($^1/_2$–1 minute less in the second stage of cooking). It too can be combined with fresh mushrooms or Chinese dried mushrooms which are soaked first.

## Plain Stir-fried Young Leeks

Young leeks can also be cooked in the same way as spinach.
When the Chinese cook leeks they use all the green part. The
leek is cut diagonally into approximately 2-inch segments.

The green parts are added to the stir-fry about a minute after
the white parts. Being a strong-tasting vegetable, it benefits
from a tablespoon or two of Vegetable Broth, added at the
second stage. For non-vegetarians, it is usually combined with
such strong-flavoured meats as beef or lamb, which are cut
into the same size as the leek and in very thin slices; these are
put into the stir-fry a minute before the leeks.

## Plain Stir-fried Celery

Although celery is a somewhat harder vegetable than the previous one, it requires no more cooking. It can be treated in the
same way as young leeks or any of the previous vegetables
(sliced diagonally into $1^1/_2$-inch segments). When cooked with
other vegetables, it is usually combined with chilli pepper to
produce a hot dish. One or two shredded red chilli peppers are
added to the stir-fry along with onion, ginger and garlic before
the celery is put into the pan. A tablespoon or two of butter
makes a welcome addition during the second stage of the
cooking. For non-vegetarians, celery can be stir-fried with
sliced pork, beef, lamb, bacon or ham, which should be stir-
fried for a minute or two ($2^1/_2$–3 minutes for pork) before the
celery is added.

## Watercress, Sea-kale, Endive

These three vegetables are used in the West mainly for salads.
However, when stir-fried they can be treated in the same
manner as celery or young leeks (see above). A tablespoon of
hoisin sauce, 1 tablespoon of peanut butter and tomato purée

can be added during the early stage of stir-frying. Cress is seldom prepared and eaten on its own. More often it is chopped and used as garnish on other vegetables and dishes. A typical case is when it is used to garnish a dish of stir-fried tomato.

### Plain Stir-fried Tomatoes
(for 4–6 portions)

| | |
|---|---|
| 8 firm medium size red tomatoes | 4-inch segment cucumber |
| 2 stalks spring onion | 2 cloves garlic |
| $1/2$ teaspoon salt | 2 slices ginger root |
| 3 tablespoons vegetable oil | 3 tablespoons soya sauce |
| 2 tablespoons butter | $1/2$ tablespoon soya paste |
| 2 teaspoons sugar | 1 tablespoon hoisin sauce |
| 2 tablespoons chopped watercress | 2 tablespoons dry sherry |

Douse the tomatoes in boiling water and skin them. Slice each tomato vertically into quarters. Slice the cucumber lengthwise into 2-inch long thin slices; do not remove the skin. Chop the spring onion, including green parts, into $1/4$-inch segments. Crush the garlic and shred the ginger.

Heat the oil in a frying-pan. When hot add the garlic, ginger and spring onion. Stir-fry for $1/2$ a minute. Add the butter and cucumber. Stir-fry for $1^1/2$ minutes. Add the tomatoes, soya sauce, soya paste, sugar and hoisin sauce. Turn gently in the oil and sauce for 2 minutes. Pour in the sherry. Turn and stir gently for another $1^1/2$ minutes. Sprinkle with chopped watercress and serve.

### Plain Stir-fried Chinese Cabbage

Chinese cabbage is now readily available in the UK, and it has already been popular in the USA for many years. In texture it lies somewhere between lettuce and celery, but it has a flavour all its own. It can be treated just like a celery, which means that it doesn't need much cooking, and it is tasty enough to stand on its own and be cooked in the same way as Plain Stir-fried Spinach (above). It is often cooked 'hot', combined with one or two shredded chilli peppers put into the oil during the early stage of the stir-fry. As an alternative, some shredded Chinese dried mushrooms (soaked) can be added, along with 1 or 2 tablespoons of butter, and 1 tablespoon of hoisin sauce, all put in at the second stage of the stir-frying.

For non-vegetarians, Chinese cabbage is often stir-fried together with thinly sliced meat ($^1/_4$–$^1/_2$ lb of pork, chicken, beef or lamb), which is added to the stir-fry a minute or two before the cabbage. The meat may require some slight seasoning ($^1/_2$ teaspoon of salt, or 1 tablespoon of soya sauce and pepper to taste) before it is put into the pan. When it has cooked for a minute or two, the meat is pushed to the sides of the pan so that the main vegetables can be stir-fried in the middle. When the latter is ready, the meats, which have been cooking longer, are scooped or stirred back into the middle to combine with the vegetable, and perhaps a spoonful or two of 'broth', soya sauce and sherry for the final stir-up. It is often at this last stage that some final adjustments in seasonings can be made, if necessary, and not infrequently some minute quantity of aromatic or enrichening oil, such as sesame oil or chicken fat, can be added to give interest and distinction to the dish. Ordinary cabbage such as Savoy can be cooked in a similar way but it will require an extra 3–4 minutes of sautéing at a low to medium heat, before a final toss and stir-up.

### *Plain Stir-fried Young Beans or Pea Pods (Mange-tout)*
(for 4–6 portions)

So long as they are young and tender French beans and pea pods can be treated in the same manner, and stir-fried with great success. Unlike spinach, leeks and celery, which are not overpowered by the strongly flavoured garlic, ginger and onion, the more delicate French beans and pea pods are best cooked largely on their own.

1 lb French beans (or pea pods)
$^1/_2$ teaspoon salt
2 tablespoons vegetable oil
4 tablespoons Vegetable Broth
1 tablespoon soya sauce
$1^1/_2$ tablespoons sherry

1 teaspoon sugar, blended in 2 tablespoons water with 1 teaspoon cornflour
$^1/_2$ teaspoon vegetable bouillon powder
$^1/_2$ tablespoon hoisin sauce
2 tablespoons butter

Wash, dry and top and tail and remove string from the beans or pea pods if necessary.

Heat the oil in a frying-pan. Add salt. Stir a few times. Add the beans or pea pods. Stir-fry gently on a moderate heat for 2 minutes. Add 'broth', butter, soya sauce, vegetable bouillon powder and continue to stir-fry gently for 3 minutes. Add sugar blended with cornflour and water, and sherry. Stir and turn the vegetables for a further minute and serve. Because the stir-frying here is gentle the process is akin to and can be described as sautéing.

*Alternative Combinations*: For such a pure dish of glistening green, the only extraneous element which can be introduced without distracting from its purity is the dark brown richness of Chinese dried black mushrooms. These must be soaked and their stems removed. Then about 6–8 pieces are added initially along with the beans, a tablespoon of extra oil, and $^1/_2$ tablespoon of extra butter. They are then stirred and cooked gently together with the beans in the course of the next 6–8 minutes.

This dish is not suited to the addition of any meat, but concentrated chicken broth might be substituted for Vegetable

Broth. On the other hand, beans or pea pods prepared in this way can be used to garnish dishes which are mainly meat.

### Plain Stir-fried Green Peas
(for 4–6 portions)

| | |
|---|---|
| 1 lb fresh green peas (or frozen) | 3 tablespoons butter |
| 4 Chinese dried black mushrooms | 4 tablespoons Vegetable Broth |
| 2 oz bamboo-shoots | $^1/_2$ teaspoon vegetable bouillon powder |
| 1 tablespoon dried bean-curd (tofu) (optional) | $^1/_2$ teaspoon tofu cheese |
| $^1/_2$ teaspoon salt | 1 tablespoon soya sauce |
| 2 tablespoons vegetable oil | 2 teaspoons sugar |
| | 1 tablespoon sherry |

Thaw the peas if frozen. Soak the Chinese mushrooms for $^1/_2$ an hour. Discard the stems and dice the mushrooms approximately the same size as the peas. Dice the bamboo-shoots and dried tofu into approximately the same size pieces.

Heat the butter in a frying-pan. When hot, add the salt and the peas. Stir-fry on a medium heat for 2 minutes. Meanwhile heat the oil in a separate smaller pan over a high flame. Add the diced mushrooms, bamboo-shoots and dried tofu, and stir-fry on a high heat for 2 minutes. Pour the contents of the smaller pan into the larger pan containing the peas. Add the Vegetable Broth, tofu cheese, soya sauce, vegetable bouillon powder, sugar and sherry. Stir-fry gently on a low heat for a further 4–5 minutes. Adjust for seasoning and serve.

## STIR-FRYING AND BRAISING (OR SAUTÉING)

This is simply an extension of the ordinary process of quick stir-frying in which harder vegetables are given an extra period (3–5 minutes) of braising under cover. This is usually effected by adding some additional quantity of liquid (Vegetable Broth if vegetarian, or chicken stock if not) and placing a tight-fitting lid over the frying-pan for an additional period of cooking on a low or medium heat. The heat may be raised again for the final stir-up, when the lid is removed, and small quantities of wine and aromatic oil added (or, for non-vegetarians, chicken fat or lard). It is usually the semi-hard vegetables, such as broccoli, French beans, Brussels sprouts, hard cabbage, cauliflower, chicory, peppers, aubergines, marrows, courgettes, etc., which are cooked in this way. Apart from the tenderizing effect of the somewhat longer cooking, the extra time also allows flavours of the different ingredients to mingle.

### Stir-braised Broccoli or Cauliflower
(for 6–8 portions)

1 medium/large cauliflower
  (or 2 broccolis)
1 small onion
1 slice ginger root
1 clove garlic
3 tablespoons vegetable oil
2 tablespoons butter
3 tablespoons milk
salt and pepper (to taste)
4 tablespoons Vegetable
  Broth
$1/_2$ teaspoon vegetable
  bouillon powder

Break the cauliflower or broccoli into individual florets. Chop the onion into small pieces. Shred the ginger. Crush the garlic.

Heat the oil in a frying-pan with a lid. When hot add the onion, ginger, garlic, pepper and salt to taste and stir-fry for 1 minute. Add the cauliflower and turn the pieces in the oil in a gentle stir-fry for 2 minutes. Add 'broth', butter, milk and vegetable bouillon powder and continue to stir-fry gently for 2 minutes until the butter has all melted and the vegetable is well covered with the liquid in the pan, which has begun to boil vigorously. Reduce the heat to low, and place the lid tightly over the pan. Allow the contents to simmer gently for 3–4 minutes. Uncover, adjust for seasoning, turn the vegetable around gently a couple of times, and serve. In cooking broccoli, the simmering under cover may have to continue for a couple of extra minutes.

For non-vegetarians, simply break $1/2$–1 chicken stock cube over the vegetables when the butter, broth and milk are added. In preparing more elaborate meals a few tablespoons of Fu-Yung Sauce (see page 82) may be added before serving.

### Stir-braised Brussels Sprouts (or Cabbage or French Beans)
### (for 4–6 portions)

1 lb Brussels sprouts (or medium-size cabbage or $3/4$ lb beans)
3 tablespoons vegetable oil
$1/2$ teaspoon salt
2 slices ginger root
1 clove garlic
4 tablespoons Vegetable Broth

2 tablespoons butter
$1^1/_2$ tablespoons soya sauce
$1/2$ teaspoon vegetable bouillon powder
$1/2$ tablespoon hoisin sauce
2 tablespoons sherry
$1^1/_2$ teaspoons sugar
salt and pepper (to taste)

Cut each sprout into halves or quarters; or top and tail the beans and cut them diagonally into 2-inch pieces; or remove the main stalk of the cabbage and slice it in 1-inch strips. Crush the garlic and shred the ginger.

Heat the oil in the frying-pan. Add salt, ginger and garlic, stir a few times and add the sprouts. Stir them in the oil over medium heat for 2 minutes. Add the 'broth' and stir-fry gently for 2 more minutes. Add the soya sauce, hoisin sauce, sherry, butter, sugar and vegetable bouillon powder. Turn the sprouts around two or three times. Place the lid tightly over the pan. Reduce the heat to low, and allow the contents to simmer gently for 4–5 minutes. Open the lid, turn the vegetables around a couple of times and adjust the seasoning. Serve in a bowl. For non-vegetarians, break $1/2$–1 chicken stock cube over the vegetables when the broth is added. Or for increased flavour a tablespoon or two of Ratatouille Chinoise (see page 79) or Hot Peanut Butter Sauce (see page 84) may be added before serving.

### Stir-braised Aubergine (or Courgettes or Marrows)

If cut into $1/3$–$1/2$-inch-thick slices, these vegetables can be cooked in precisely the same manner as the sprouts or cabbage in the previous recipe. Ratatouille Chinoise (see page 79) or Hot Peanut Butter Sauce (see page 84) are also effective additions to this dish.

### Stir-braised Carrots (or Asparagus or Fresh Bamboo-shoots)
(for 4–6 portions)

The one quality which these three vegetables have in common is that they are crunchy and harder than any of the previous vegetables and therefore require somewhat longer cooking. For them, the cooking order is frequently reversed: braising first, followed by stir-frying. Or sometimes they are parboiled, stir-fried, braised and finally stir-fried once more.

1 lb young carrots (or asparagus or bamboo-shoots)
$1^1/2$ teaspoons salt
3 tablespoons vegetable oil
1 slice ginger root
1 clove garlic
$1^1/2$ tablespoons soya sauce

$1/2$ cup Vegetable Broth
$1/2$ teaspoon vegetable bouillon powder
2 tablespoons butter
$1^1/2$ teaspoons sugar
1 tablespoon hoisin sauce
2 tablespoons dry sherry

Trim the vegetable and slice diagonally into $1^1/_2$–2-inch segments. Crush the garlic and shred the ginger.

Parboil the vegetable in boiling water for 5–6 minutes. Drain thoroughly. Heat the oil in a frying-pan. Add the ginger, garlic and salt. Stir for $^1/_2$ a minute. Add the vegetables and stir-fry gently on a medium heat for 5 minutes. Pour in the Vegetable Broth, soya sauce, hoisin sauce, and add the vegetable bouillon powder. Stir the contents around a few times. Place the lid on the pan tightly and leave the contents to simmer for 10–12 minutes. Open the lid, add the butter, sugar and sherry and raise the heat to high. Stir-fry gently until the liquid in the pan is thick and has almost dried up. Serve immediately.

*Note:* Asparagus, carrot and bamboo-shoots can all benefit from the addition of $^1/_2$ dozen medium-sized Chinese dried mushrooms, which are first soaked in hot water, then cut into thin slices and added along with the Vegetable Broth.

# Deep-fry and Stir-fry

This double method of cooking is often used in combining hard and semi-hard vegetables with soft vegetables in one dish. The hard and semi-hard vegetables are deep-fried for a period, and then combined with the stir-fried soft vegetables. The flavourers (seasonings and sauces) are applied only during the second stage of the cooking. For instance, the hard vegetables in the preceding recipe – carrots, asparagus, bamboo-shoots or turnips – can be combined with Chinese cabbage and dried mushrooms very successfully in this way.

### *Deep-fried Carrots, Asparagus and Bamboo-shoots and Quick-fried Chinese Cabbage and Mushrooms Casserole*
(for 4–6 portions)

$^1/_3$ lb young carrots
$^1/_3$ lb asparagus
$^1/_3$ lb bamboo-shoots
$^1/_2$ lb Chinese cabbage (or ordinary cabbage)
6 large Chinese dried mushrooms
2 tablespoons soya sauce
1 tablespoon soya paste
1 tablespoon hoisin sauce

2 teaspoons sugar
$^1/_2$ teaspoon vegetable bouillon powder
4 tablespoons Vegetable Broth
2 tablespoons dry sherry
2 tablespoons butter
2 teaspoons sesame oil
$^1/_2$ teaspoon salt
oil for deep-frying

Remove the coarse part of the asparagus and trim the carrots and bamboo-shoots to the same thickness as the asparagus, cutting them into about 1–2-inch segments. Soak the dried mushrooms for $^1/_2$ an hour in hot water, discard stalks and shred the mushrooms. Cut the cabbage into 1-inch slices.

Place the carrots, asparagus and bamboo-shoots in a wire basket and deep-fry in hot oil for 6–7 minutes; drain thoroughly.

Meanwhile heat the butter and sesame oil in a casserole. When the butter has melted, add the mushrooms, stir for $^1/_2$ a minute, and add the cabbage and salt. Stir-fry gently for 3–4 minutes on a medium heat. Add the deep-fried vegetables and the flavourers, along with the Vegetable Broth and sherry. Turn the heat from medium to high. Stir and turn the vegetables together for 2–3 minutes and serve in the casserole.

## The Monk's Mixed Vegetable Ensemble
(for 4–6 portions)

The Monk's Vegetable Ensemble is a well-known dish in China. It can be prepared by repeating the previous recipe (almost any other hard vegetable can take the place of asparagus or it can be omitted altogether, if not in season or hard to obtain: Chinese cooking is usually very flexible) and adding three other items:

| | |
|---|---|
| 1 or 2 cakes tofu | 2 oz lily bud stalks ('golden |
| 4 oz transparent pea-starch | needles') |
| noodles | |

You will also need double the quantity of soya sauce (2 tablespoons) and vegetable bouillon powder (1 teaspoon) and three times as much Vegetable Broth (12 tablespoons).

The tofu is cut into 1-inch cubes and deep-fried for 2–3 minutes, along with the hard vegetables. The pea-starch noodles are soaked and softened in hot water for 5 minutes and drained. The lily bud stalks are cut into 2-inch-long segments and soaked in hot water for $^1/_2$ an hour with the dried mushrooms (the cup of water used for soaking the two items should be retained for adding to the whole ensemble when all the vegetables are combined together). When these three items are prepared, they are added with all the other vegetables to the casserole along with the mushroom/lily-bud stalk water. At this point the liquid may be thickened with 1–2 teaspoons of cornflour. The tender parts of spring greens, i.e. the heart and fresh leaves, can be used instead of or along with cabbage or Chinese cabbage, or celery. The whole amalgam of vegetables should be allowed to cook gently for 10 minutes under cover in the casserole. When ready, the vegetables should be sprinkled with 1–2 tablespoons of sherry and an extra 2 teaspoons of sesame oil, and served. The lily bud stalks give a very Chinese type of marshy flavour, which is an acquired taste, reminding the Chinese very much of the Good Earth and the Old Ancestral Country.

## Quick Deep-fried and Stir-fried Mixed Vegetables
(for 4–6 portions)

If you have a deep-fryer handy, you can combine the two methods of cooking into one quick process. As is apparent at this stage of the book, in Chinese cooking different cooking methods are often combined or telescoped not just to tenderize the food (which is of course part of it) but also to facilitate the amalgamation of flavours – flavours which sometimes arise only through the different methods of cooking themselves.

$^1/_2$ lb tender heart of spring
   greens
$^1/_2$ lb cabbage
$^1/_4$ lb bamboo-shoots
$^1/_4$ lb bean sprouts
$^1/_3$ lb spinach
2 cloves garlic
2 slices ginger root

1 teaspoon salt
2 tablespoons soya sauce
1 tablespoon hoisin sauce
$^1/_2$ teaspoon vegetable
   bouillon powder
4 tablespoons Vegetable
   Broth
2 tablespoons dry sherry

2 tablespoons butter                    oil for deep-frying
1 tablespoon sesame oil

Clean and cut the spring greens, cabbage and bamboo-shoots into $1\frac{1}{2}$–2-inch pieces. Wash and dry the spinach and remove the tougher stems. Crush the garlic and shred the ginger.

Heat the oil in the deep-fryer. When hot, place the greens, cabbage and bamboo-shoots in a wire basket and deep-fry for 3 minutes. Drain. Heat the butter and sesame oil in a large frying-pan. Add the salt, garlic and ginger. Stir them around in the oil for $\frac{1}{2}$ a minute. Add the sprouts and spinach, and stir-fry on a high heat for 2 minutes. Add all the other vegetables, seasonings and the flavourers. Stir-fry them together still on a high heat for 3 minutes, sprinkle with sherry and serve.

For a full appreciation of the flavour, this dish should be eaten immediately.


### Quick Deep-fried Cauliflower and Heart of Spring Greens (in batter) with Stir-fried Seasonal Vegetables
(for 4–5 portions)

Seasonable vegetables can be $\frac{1}{4}$ lb bean sprouts, $\frac{1}{4}$ lb fresh mushrooms and 2 oz spring bamboo-shoots. This recipe differs from the previous one in that the cauliflower and heart of spring greens ($\frac{1}{4}$–$\frac{1}{2}$ lb of each) are deep-fried in a light batter (1 egg white beaten together with 3 tablespoons of flour and 4 tablespoons of milk for $\frac{1}{4}$ of a minute with a rotary beater). The cauliflower is broken into $1\frac{1}{2}$–2-inch florets and the greens cut into the same size pieces. They are dipped in the batter and deep-fried for 3–4 minutes, then drained. The mushrooms and bamboo-shoots, which are cut into very thin slices, are stir-fried in 4 tablespoons of butter impregnated with small quantities of chopped garlic and onion for just a minute. The two groups of vegetables are mixed together and stir-fried. All the various seasonings and flavourers (the same as in the previous recipe) are added to this final stir-fry, which takes no more than 2–3 minutes on a high heat. Because the cooking time is so short, the 'seasonal vegetables' are very crisp, providing a contrasting surface texture for the vegetables cooked in batter, which are still crunchy underneath. Sometimes the vegetables in batter are given a brief stir-fry and $1/2$–1 teaspoon of chilli sauce is added along with a little additional soya sauce, sugar and oil before they are combined with the other vegetables in the final stir-fry.

### Quick Deep-fried Aubergine (and/or Courgettes) with Stir-fried Seasonal Vegetables
(for 4–6 portions)

Aubergine and courgettes can be treated in exactly the same manner as cauliflower or hearts of spring greens of the previous recipe: that is, they can be cut into 1–2-inch pieces, lightly dipped in batter and then deep-fried for 3–4 minutes, drained, and followed by a very short period of stir-frying in 1–2 tablespoons of sesame oil and 1 teaspoon of chilli sauce, before being combined with the unbattered seasonal vegetables for the final stir-fry together with the addition of the usual range of seasonings and flavourers: namely, salt, soya sauce, hoisin sauce, vegetable bouillon powder, Vegetable Broth, sugar and sherry, after the seasonal vegetables have been treated to a minute's stir-frying in 2 tablespoons of butter. The seasonings and flavourers employed can be of the same quantities as in the recipe Quick Deep-fried and Stir-fried Mixed Vegetables if about $1/2$ lb each of aubergine or courgettes are used. The touch of chilli sauce adds a slight liveliness to the dish.

Alternatively, unbattered aubergine can be quickly stir-fried with finely chopped spring onions, garlic and fresh ginger, with the usual seasonings.

34

*Quick Deep-fried and Stir-fried Chinese Cabbage or Tender
Hearts of Savoy Cabbage or Spring Greens)*
(for 4–6 portions)

When the vegetables are in season and particularly fresh, they
can be treated to cooking in this manner without their being
combined with or 'married' to other vegetables. When cooked
on their own, the cabbage should be very fresh and tender, or
if Savoy cabbage or spring greens are used, only the tenderest
parts of the hearts of the vegetable should be used.

1 lb young Chinese cabbage
 (or tender hearts of Savoy
 cabbage or spring greens)
vegetable oil for deep-frying
2 tablespoons sesame oil for
 stir-fry
1 clove garlic
1 slice ginger root
$^1/_2$ teaspoon salt
$1^1/_2$ tablespoons soya sauce

$^1/_2$ teaspoon vegetable
 bouillon powder
4 tablespoons Vegetable
 Broth
$1^1/_2$ teaspoons sugar
pepper (to taste)
2 tablespoons sherry
$^1/_2$ tablespoon cornflour
 blended in 3 tablespoons
 water

Cut the cabbage across the stems into 2–3-inch-wide pieces.
Blend the cornflour and water mixture with the Vegetable
Broth in a bowl with the vegetable bouillon powder. Crush the
garlic and ginger.

Deep-fry the cabbage (or Savoy or spring greens) in hot oil
for 2 minutes and quickly drain. Heat the sesame oil in a
frying-pan. Add the ginger and garlic and stir-fry for $^1/_2$
a minute over moderate heat. Add the cabbage and stir-fry for
2 minutes. Add the salt, pepper and soya sauce and stir-fry
together for 1 minute. Add the cornflour, 'broth' and vegetable
bouillon powder mixture, sugar and sherry and continue to
stir-fry for $1^1/_2$ minutes and serve. As the cabbage (or Savoy or
greens) is here to cook largely on its own, with only the assist-
ance of seasonings and flavourers, the appeal of the dish lies

35

largely in bringing out the native taste and flavour of the vegetable itself, which in the mixture of savouriness of a Chinese meal often stands out for its purity.

### Quick Deep-fried and Stir-fried Sweet and Sour Chinese Cabbage (or Savoy Cabbage or Spring Greens)

The difference between this dish and the previous is that it does not use only the tenderest parts of the vegetable: much of the coarser leaves can be included. The procedure is exactly the same as in the preceding recipe, except during the final stir-fry, after all the seasonings and flavourers have been added, 5–6 tablespoons of Sweet and Sour Sauce (see page 81) are added and the stir-frying extended for $1^1/_2$–2 minutes. The extra time in cooking helps both to tenderize the coarser parts of the vegetable and to give the sauce a chance to flavour and penetrate the vegetable. This recipe is more suitable than the previous one when the vegetables available are not of prime quality.

### Quick Deep-fried Celery with Stir-fried Red Pepper and Hot-pickled Szechuan Cabbage
(for 5–6 portions)

Hot-pickled Szechuan cabbage has almost the effect of curry in that it is 'hot' and therefore blankets or camouflages most other flavours. But when used discreetly and in small quantities it enhances and brings out the flavours of the other ingredients (this is applicable to meats as well as to vegetables).

| | |
|---|---|
| 1 lb celery (or broccoli) | 2 tablespoons soya sauce |
| 1 medium-size red sweet pepper | $1^1/_2$ teaspoons sugar |
| | 3 tablespoons Hot Black |

| | |
|---|---|
| 1–2 oz hot-pickled Szechuan cabbage | Beans and Tomato Sauce (see page 79) |
| 2 tablespoons sesame oil (or butter) | oil for deep-frying |
| 3 tablespoons Vegetable Broth | |

Clean the celery (or broccoli) and cut diagonally into 1-inch segments. Slice the pepper and Szechuan cabbage into thin strips.

Place the celery in a wire basket and deep-fry in hot oil for 2 minutes; drain. Heat the seasame oil or butter in a large frying-pan. When hot, add the red pepper and Szechuan cabbage. Stir-fry quickly on a high heat for $1^1/_2$ minutes. Add the celery. Stir, toss and mix the vegetables together for 2 minutes. Add the soya sauce, Vegetable Broth, sugar and Black Beans and Tomato Sauce. Stir, scramble, toss for a further 2 minutes and serve.

### Quick Deep-fried and Stir-fried French Beans
(for 5–6 portions)

French beans can be cooked in a similar fashion to the preceding recipes, but since they are more subtle in flavour, they are best cooked on their own, rather than in combination with other vegetables.

| | |
|---|---|
| 1 lb young French beans | 2 tablespoons Vegetable Broth |
| oil for deep-frying | |
| 2 cloves garlic | 1 teaspoon sugar |
| $1^1/_2$ tablespoons soya sauce | $1^1/_2$ tablespoons sherry |
| 1 tablespoon hoisin sauce | 2 tablespoons butter |

Wash and dry the beans. Top and tail if necessary. Crush the garlic.

Heat the oil in the deep-fryer. When very hot place the beans in a wire basket. Deep-fry the beans in two lots for 2 minutes and drain. Heat the butter in a frying-pan. Add the garlic, soya sauce, hoisin sauce and Vegetable Broth. Stir them together on a medium heat for 1 minute. Add the beans, turn the heat up to high. Add the sherry and sugar. Turn the beans around in the sauce for $2^1/_2$ minutes and serve.

### Quick Deep-fried and Quick-fried Button Mushrooms
(for 4–5 portions)

This is a Yanchow dish, from the northern bank of the Yangtze, and is considered a delicacy.

$1^1/_4$ lb large button
   mushrooms
oil for deep-frying
1 tablespoon cornflour
$1/_2$ teaspoon vegetable
   bouillon powder
3 tablespoons Vegetable
   Broth

2 egg whites
2 tablespoons sesame oil (or
   butter)
3 teaspoons sea salt
$1^1/_2$ teaspoons freshly ground
   pepper

Remove the stems from the mushrooms. Wash and dry. Mix the cornflour, vegetable bouillon powder, Vegetable Broth and egg whites together in a bowl. Beat them together for 10–15 seconds with a fork until well blended. Dip the mushrooms and cover with this batter. Heat and stir the sea salt and pepper in a small and very dry pan over low heat for 3 minutes until it develops a 'bouquet' (this is the Roasted Aromatic Salt and Pepper Mix – see page 40).

Heat the oil in the deep-fryer. When hot place the batter-covered mushrooms in a wire basket and deep-fry them for $2^1/_2$ minutes and drain. Heat the sesame oil or butter in a frying-pan. When hot add the mushrooms, turn them gently in the oil for 2 minutes. Leave to sauté for 2 minutes. Take a pinch or two of the aromatic salt and pepper mixture, sprinkle it lightly over the mushrooms and serve.

# PLAIN DEEP-FRYING

Although deep-frying as a cooking process for vegetables is more often than not used in conjunction with other processes (as we have seen in the preceding recipes), it can sometimes be used independently quite successfully.

### *Deep-fried Marinaded Mushrooms*
(for 4–6 portions)

1½ lb medium-size button
    mushrooms (must be
    firm)

**FOR BATTER**

2 eggs
½ cup plain flour

¼ cup milk
oil for deep-frying

**FOR MARINADE**

2 tablespoons soya sauce
½ tablespoon hoisin sauce
½ tablespoon light soya
    sauce
1 tablespoon vinegar
1 tablespoon sherry

2 teaspoons sugar
¼ teaspoon vegetable
    bouillon powder
1½ teaspoons chilli sauce
2 tablespoons Vegetable
    Broth

Clean the mushrooms thoroughly and remove the stems. Beat the ingredients for the batter together with a rotary beater for 1 minute. Mix the ingredients for the marinade in a bowl. Add the mushrooms to the marinade and leave for 1 hour. Drain thoroughly.

Dip each mushroom in the batter and drain off any excess batter. Place 4–5 mushrooms in a wire basket (or use a perforated spoon) to deep-fry for 3 minutes. Repeat until all the mushrooms have been deep-fried and well drained.

The deep-fried mushrooms can be served as they are, or they can be served with any one of the following sauces:

Mushroom Sauce (page 82)
Hot Black Beans and Tomato Sauce (page 79)
Fu-Yung Sauce (page 82)
Hot Peanut Butter Sauce (page 84)

or they can be served with Roasted Aromatic Salt and Pepper Mix (stir-fry gently 2 teaspoons of pepper with 1 tablespoon of sea salt for 2–3 minutes on a completely dry pan over gentle heat, until a 'bouquet' arises), which should be used as a dip.

### Deep-fried Marinaded Cauliflower, Broccoli, Bamboo-shoots, Asparagus, Aubergine, Brussels Sprouts, etc.

Any one of the above vegetables can be treated in the same manner as the mushrooms in the previous recipe, except that since they are harder vegetables they require an extra minute of deep-frying. Cooked in this way, and served with appropriate sauce or dips, they can be very successful as starters (at a Western meal) or they can simply be served on their own as one of the several dishes in a Chinese multi-course or multi-dish meal. The difference in their textures makes them interesting dishes to serve along with other stir-fried or clear-simmered dishes.

# Steaming

Because of the nature of Chinese cooking, one method often runs into another, or into several others. Only occasionally does one type of cooking stand entirely alone. Steaming is often used in China either as an initial process, to soften some of the tougher ingredients, or as a concluding one, to 'seal' together the various ingredients; it may also be used as a single process, where the cooking is best maintained at an even temperature, with no risk of the dish drying up or getting burnt. Steaming is more widely used in cooking in China than in the West because in the cooking of rice (usually in huge quantities) a great deal of steam is produced, and this steam is often utilized as part of the cooking process. The aim of steaming is usually to produce 'pure' dishes, that is, dishes which do not contain much sauce or heavy seasoning but rely more on the inherent flavour of the main ingredient. As food is usually steamed in the dishes in which it is served, the prepared dishes are often placed in a many-tiered bamboo steam-basket over the cooking rice. Sometimes, to keep them hot, dishes are steamed just before they are brought to the table. Almost any dish cooked by another method can be steamed for a short period without losing any of its essential qualities. Hence a brief, brisk period of steaming to 'seal' the dish is a common practice in China. Longer periods of steaming in a covered vessel is a method usually reserved for the 'pudding' dishes – in other words, dishes which are packed into a large heatproof bowl or basin, steamed for a prolonged period, then tipped out on to a serving dish, a method more frequently used for meat than for vegetables. This long steaming is equivalent to cooking in a double-boiler. For medium periods of steaming, the dishes which are cooked in this manner are usually the 'assembled' ones – that is, foods which have been prepared, cooked and flavoured in different ways are assembled in one heatproof bowl or in a casserole, and steamed together for a time.

### Quick-steamed Buttered Lettuce (or Chinese Cabbage)
(for 4–6 portions)

2–3 heads Cos lettuce (about 1 lb)
3 tablespoons butter
1 teaspoon salt
pepper (to taste)
4 tablespoons Vegetable Broth
1 tablespoon light soya sauce
1 teaspoon cornflour blended in 2 tablespoons water
$1/4$ teaspoon vegetable bouillon powder
$1^1/_2$ teaspoons sugar
2 tablespoons beer (Guinness) or 1 tablespoon sherry

Remove the root and coarser leaves of the lettuce. Cut the remaining leaves across the stem into 2–3-inch segments. Blend the cornflour mixture with the Vegetable Broth.

Heat the butter in a large frying-pan. When hot and melted, add the lettuce, spread it out, and stir and turn until the vegetable is well covered with the oil. Sprinkle with salt and add all the other ingredients. Turn and stir them together with the lettuce for $1/2$ a minute. Turn out on to a heatproof dish, pouring the gravy over the lettuce. Place the dish in a steamer and steam vigorously for 3–4 minutes, then serve.

### Quick-steamed Buttered Pea Pods (or Mange-tout)
(for 4–6 portions)

Pea pods can be cooked in precisely the same way as lettuce in the preceding recipe, except in the final cooking the steaming can be extended for an extra minute. A clove of garlic and a slice of ginger may be added to the oil, or butter, in the initial frying stage for just a touch of their flavour (they should be removed when the dish is served).

### Steamed Broccoli with Fu-Yung Sauce
(for 4–6 portions)

| | |
|---|---|
| 1 lb broccoli | 4 tablespoons Vegetable Broth |
| 1 clove garlic | 1 tablespoon butter |
| 2 slices ginger root | $^1/_2$ teaspoon vegetable bouillon powder |
| 3 tablespoons vegetable oil | |
| 1 teaspoon salt | 1 tablespoon light soya sauce |
| $^1/_2$ tablespoon bean-curd (tofu) cheese | 6 tablespoons Fu-Yung Sauce (see page 82) |

Cut the broccoli into 2–3-inch pieces, or break into branches. Crush the garlic and shred the ginger.

Heat the oil in a large frying-pan. When hot, add the garlic and ginger and stir together for $^1/_2$ a minute. Add the broccoli, sprinkle with salt, and turn in the oil until every piece is well covered. Add the butter, Vegetable Broth, vegetable bouillon powder, soya sauce and tofu cheese. Stir-fry them all together for 2 minutes on a medium heat. Add the Fu-Yung Sauce, spread it over the broccoli, and empty the contents of the pan into a heatproof dish. Place the dish in a steamer and steam vigorously for 5–6 minutes. Serve in the dish.

*Note:* Young leeks or cauliflower can be cooked in exactly the same manner. For non-vegetarians, the Vegetable Broth can be replaced with 4–5 tablespoons of concentrated chicken broth.

### Steamed Cabbage and Spring Greens (with stem)
(for 4–6 portions)

Chinese vegetarians consider the hard stems of various vegetables as delicacies when they are properly prepared and cooked.

| | |
|---|---|
| 1 medium-size cabbage (Savoy) | 2 slices ginger root |
| $^3/_4$ lb spring greens | 1 clove garlic |
| $^1/_2$ lb cabbage and spring green stems | 1 stalk spring onion |
| 1 teaspoon salt | 2 teaspoons salt |
| $^1/_2$ pint Vegetable Broth | 2 tablespoons vegetable oil |
| $^1/_2$ teaspoon vegetable bouillon powder | 1 tablespoon soya sauce |
| | $1^1/_2$ teaspoons sugar |
| | 1 tablespoon butter |
| | 1 tablespoon hoisin sauce |

Remove the leaves from the stems of the cabbage and greens. Cut or carve the stems into neat bite-size pieces. Parboil them in boiling water for 3–4 minutes to remove any bitterness. Select the fresher leaves of the vegetables and slice them into 2–3-inch pieces. Crush the garlic and shred the ginger. Cut the spring onion into 1-inch segments.

Place the stem pieces at the bottom of a large heatproof bowl. Sprinkle with salt. Pour in the 'broth' and add the vegetable bouillon powder and sugar. Cover the bowl with greaseproof paper, place the bowl in a steamer and steam for 40 minutes.

Meanwhile heat the oil in a frying-pan and add the ginger, garlic and onion. Add the remaining salt and stir-fry for $^1/_2$ a minute. Add the butter, cabbage and greens, soya sauce and hoisin sauce. Stir-fry them all together for about 2 minutes, or until the vegetables are well covered with the oil and flavourers. Put the stir-fried vegetables on top of the ingredients in the heatproof bowl, and steam vigorously for a further 4–5 minutes. Serve in the bowl. This dish is almost a soup; the diners will find the roots of the vegetables are at least as appealing as the freshly fried leaves (and to some, more satisfying).

## Plain Steamed Chinese Mushrooms (dried)
(for 6–8 portions)

This dish, another semi-soup, is considered a delicacy and is often served during a banquet – its simplicity contrasting with the more elaborately prepared dishes.

20 selected Chinese dried
   mushrooms (of about
   even size, weighing about
   $1/_3$–$1/_2$ lb before soaking)
$1/_2$ pint Vegetable Broth
$1^1/_2$ tablespoons light soya
   sauce

$1/_2$ teaspoon vegetable
   bouillon powder
$1/_2$ teaspoon salt
1 teaspoon sugar
2 slices ginger root
2 stalks spring onion

Soak the mushrooms in 1 pint of hot water for 1 hour, and remove and discard the stems. Cut the spring onion into 3–4-inch length segments, including green parts.

Place the mushrooms at the bottom of the large heatproof glass bowl. Sprinkle with the soya sauce, vegetable bouillon powder, salt and sugar and place the spring onion and ginger on top. Pour in the broth. Tie a piece of greaseproof paper over the top of the bowl. Place the bowl in a steamer and steam for 1 hour. Remove the ginger and onion, then replace the bowl in the steamer and steam for a further 10 minutes. Serve in the bowl.

## Steamed Marrow Bowl
(for 6–8 portions)

1 large marrow
4–5 large dried Chinese mushrooms
$1/_2$ cup Chinese 'grass-mushrooms' (similar in size to small button mushrooms, but more pointed in shape; usually available in tins, but small button mushrooms can be used instead)

2 teaspoons chopped Chinese pickled greens (Red-in-Snow)

4 oz heart of spring greens

$^1/_2$ teaspoon salt

2 tablespoons gingko nuts (or peanuts)

$^1/_2$ pint Vegetable Broth

1 tablespoon butter

$^1/_2$ teaspoon vegetable bouillon powder

1 tablespoon light soya sauce

2 slices ginger root

2 tablespoons sherry

Slice 8 inches off the larger end of the marrow to use as a lid, and sit the remaining part firmly in a heatproof bowl. Scoop out the inside, leaving a shell of at least $^1/_2$–$^3/_4$-inch thick. Dice some of the 'meat' from the middle portion of the marrow into $^1/_2$–1-inch cubes (about 6–7 oz). Soak the dried mushrooms in hot water for $^1/_2$ an hour, remove and discard the stems, and slice into thin strips. Boil the gingko nuts or peanuts for 10 minutes and drain. Heat the 'broth' until it begins to boil.

Place the marrow cubes, 'grass-mushrooms', nuts and heart of greens in the scooped-out cavity of the marrow. Sprinkle with soya sauce and vegetable bouillon powder and chopped Red-in-Snow. Pour in the 'broth'. Heat the butter in a frying-pan. When hot, stir-fry the sliced mushroom strips in it for 2 minutes. Place the mushroom strips on top of the other contents of the Marrow Bowl. Add the 2 pieces of ginger. Close the Marrow Bowl with the lid. Place the heatproof bowl in a steamer and steam for 1 hour. Add the sherry and steam for a further 3 minutes. Remove the 2 pieces of ginger and bring the bowl to the table, lifting the lid just before serving.

Non-vegetarians can use chicken stock instead of the Vegetable Broth and a small amount of dried prawns can be added with the other ingredients during the early stage of the cooking. Some fresh shrimps and diced chicken cubes can be added along with the sherry.

## Steamed 'Tip-Out' Vegetable Ensemble
### (for 6–8 portions)

Chinese 'tip-out' dishes are cooked and served like puddings. They are cooked in deep heatproof bowls or basins, and when ready are tipped-out on to serving dishes and served. An assortment of vegetables and other ingredients are usually packed into the basin, with the more piquant and stronger tasting ones on top; this allows their flavour to percolate through the basin in the course of the cooking. Any excess of stock or gravy is absorbed by the transparent pea-starch noodles, which are great liquid absorbers but never become soft and mushy however long they are cooked.

$^1/_4$-$^1/_2$ lb selected stems of cabbage and greens
$^1/_4$-$^1/_2$ lb broccoli and cauliflower
3 oz button mushrooms
6 large Chinese dried mushrooms
2 courgettes
1 medium-size aubergine
4 oz transparent pea-starch noodles (before soaking)
1 bean-curd (tofu) cake
2 tablespoons Chinese pickled greens (Red-in-Snow)

2 tablespoons butter
1 tablespoon hoisin sauce
$^1/_2$ tablespoon bean-curd (tofu) cheese
2 tablespoons light soya sauce
$^1/_2$ teaspoon salt
pepper (to taste)
$^1/_2$ teaspoon vegetable bouillon powder
$^1/_2$ pint Vegetable Broth
2 tablespoons sherry
oil for deep-frying

Cut the stems of the cabbage and greens into 1–1$^1/_2$-inch pieces, discarding any unsightly parts. Break the cauliflower and broccoli into individual florets and branches. Rub the inside of a large heatproof basin with butter, and press the pieces of greens, cabbage, cauliflower and broccoli against the walls of the basin. Soak the transparent noodles in warm water for 5 minutes. Drain and mix them with the button mushrooms and pour them into the basin. Sprinkle over them 2 tablespoons of soya sauce. Slice the courgettes and aubergine into $1/2$-inch-thick slices, and the tofu cake into 8 pieces. Place them in a wire basket and deep-fry them together for 3 minutes. Drain and place them on top of the noodles. Sprinkle the contents with salt, pepper, vegetable bouillon powder, hoisin sauce, tofu cheese, sherry and finely chopped Red-in-Snow. Finally, pour in the Vegetable Broth.

Tie a sheet of greaseproof paper (or aluminium foil) over the top of the basin. Place the basin in a steamer and steam steadily for 1 hour. By this time all the liquid in the basin will have been absorbed by the noodles.

Remove the greaseproof paper or foil. Tip the contents of the basin on to a well-heated, deep-sided dish and serve. The steaming mound of mixed vegetables is a most appetizing sight.

### Steamed Bean-Curd with Peanut Butter Sauce
(for 4–5 portions)

3 cakes tofu
3 tablespoons sesame paste
 (or peanut butter)
3 tablespoons sesame oil
3 tablespoons soya sauce
1 teaspoon vinegar
1 teaspoon chilli sauce
2 tablespoons sherry
1 teaspoon sugar

Cut each tofu cake into 8 pieces and place these in a heatproof dish. Place the dish in the steamer and steam vigorously for 10 minutes. Heat all the other ingredients in a small saucepan on a gentle heat, stirring continuously for $2^1/_2$ minutes. Pour the hot sauce evenly over the tofu and serve.

## Steamed Parsnips and Carrots in Hot Peanut Butter Sauce
(for 5–6 portions)

$^3/_4$ lb young carrots
$^3/_4$ lb baby parsnips
3 tablespoons butter
2 sprays parsley
FOR SAUCE
2 tablespoons sesame paste (or 3 tablespoons peanut butter)
2 tablespoons sesame oil

2 tablespoons soya sauce
2 teaspoons sugar
2 teaspoons chilli sauce (or 1 teaspoon Chinese chilli oil)
2 tablespoons sherry
1 tablespoon tomato purée
2 tablespoons Vegetable Broth

Trim, scrape and clean the carrots and parsnips. Cut diagonally into 2–3-inch segments. Chop the parsley finely. Mix the sauce mixture in a small heavy saucepan.

Heat the butter in a frying-pan. When it has melted, turn the carrots and parsnips in the butter a few times and transfer them to a large open heatproof dish. Place the latter in a steamer and steam for 45 minutes.

Meanwhile heat the sauce mixture gently on a low heat. Stir continuously for $2^1/_2$ minutes until the ingredients are well blended.

Pour the sauce evenly over the carrots and parsnips, sprinkle with chopped parsley and serve.

## Steamed French Beans in Hot Peanut Butter Sauce
(for 5–6 portions)

French beans can be prepared in the same manner as the carrots and parsnips in the previous recipe: turn them in butter, steam them for 30 minutes, and pour the prepared Hot Peanut Butter Sauce over them. No parsley is required for French beans and the quantities of ingredients for the sauce should be reduced by about one-third.

49

# Hot-marinading

Hot-marinading (Lu) is a cooking process which is perhaps peculiar to the Chinese. It consists of marinading or heating the ingredients in a master sauce, or master marinade, for a period of time and then preparing them for serving; either simply by slicing them into suitably sized pieces, or cooking them quickly by stir-frying, deep-frying, roasting, grilling or steaming; or by combining them with other foods which have been prepared and cooked in other ways. Quite often foods which have been hot-marinaded – especially meats – are simply left to cool, and then sliced for serving cold. Many items which make up the Chinese hors d'oeuvre are prepared in this manner. In the case of hot-marinaded vegetables, they are more often quickly stir-fried or deep-fried before serving, to give them a final sealing of ingredients. Without this final sealing, vegetables which are just boiled are often insipid. Although vegetables which have been hot-marinaded in a master sauce are vastly superior in taste to vegetables which have simply been boiled, a brisk dip in hot oil – even though only a small quantity – together with some final adjustments in flavour and aromatic ingredients often improves their taste immeasurably. Since hot-marinading is usually a comparatively slow process, it often allows harder vegetables time to cook through and tenderize before being mixed with some softer vegetables in a short period of stir-frying.

Frequently the root or stem of the vegetables are cut up and hot-marinaded before they are reunited with their leaves during stir-frying. Thus hot-marinading, like Chinese methods of cooking, can be employed as a single process on its own, but is more often used in conjunction with other processes. And here too one method runs into another. In Chinese cooking it is through 'marriage' and 'inter-marriage', or even 're-marriage', that the best results are achieved!

## THE MASTER SAUCE

The Master Sauce used in hot-marinading is made from familiar ingredients: soya sauce, soya paste, sherry, sugar, salt, onion, ginger root, anise, five-spice powder and peppercorn, and the foods which have been cooked in it. For non-vegetarians, the 'sauce' usually begins by making a red-cooked dish of chicken, duck, beef, lamb or pork. A panful of sauce is brought to the boil, and large pieces of meat, or whole birds, allowed to simmer slowly in it for 1 hour or more. The meat or poultry is then removed for serving and the sauce reserved for further use. The more foods that have been cooked in the sauce, the richer and more complex it becomes and the better base for further cooking. After each cooking the sauce should be skimmed and strained. If five-spice powder and anise are difficult to obtain, a bag or two of bouquet garni can be substituted. The sauce is kept 'alive' by cooking fresh materials in it at least once a week; between times it should be kept in a refrigerator. In vegetarian cooking the sauce is best started by cooking two or more lots of hard vegetables in it with one lot of semi-hard vegetables, one after another, such as carrots, haricot beans and turnips with aubergines (carrots, beans and turnips for 45 minutes, and aubergines for 25 minutes), or carrots and sweetcorn or dried beans with French beans (the first two vegetables for 40 minutes and French beans for 25 minutes). The vegetarian Master Sauce is less stable than the non-vegetarian variety as more water is released by the vegetables during cooking. To keep it 'alive', it is best to use it at least twice a week and it should be well strained through cheesecloth and skimmed after each cooking. It should always be kept in a refrigerator.

The following are the quantities for 3 pints of vegetarian Master Sauce:

### Master Sauce

1½ pints Vegetable Broth
½ pint soya sauce
¼ pint dry sherry
2 tablespoons soya paste
2 tablespoons hoisin sauce
3 tablespoons sugar
6 slices ginger root
4 medium-size onions (sliced)
2 cloves garlic (crushed)
2 bags bouquet garni (or
⅓ teaspoon five-spice powder and ¼ teaspoon ground peppercorn)
3 oz dried mushrooms
¼ lb carrots
¼ lb turnips
¼ lb peanuts
¼ lb dried beans
¼ lb runner beans (optional)
1 pint water

Soak dried beans overnight and drain. Scrape and clean the carrots and turnips. Cut diagonally into 2-inch pieces. Soak the dried mushrooms for ½ an hour in a cup of hot water.

Place the liquids, including the mushroom water, onions, sugar, garlic and spices in a heavy pan and bring to the boil. Add the dried beans, runner beans, mushrooms, peanuts, carrots and turnips and simmer very gently for 1½ hours. Remove the vegetables and strain the 'sauce' through cheesecloth; it is now ready for use. When using the sauce for hot-marinading, keep the pan at a very slow simmer.

### Hot-marinaded Stir-fried French Beans
(for 4–5 portions)

¾ lb French beans
Master Sauce
2 tablespoons butter
1 tablespoon sherry

1 clove garlic

Hot-marinade the beans for $^1/_2$ an hour in the Master Sauce.
Crush the garlic and add it to the melted butter in a frying-pan,
placed on a medium heat. Turn and stir around a few times.
Thoroughly drain the beans, add to the frying-pan, and stir-fry
for $1^1/_2$ minutes. Add the sherry and continue to stir-fry for
another minute before serving.

### Hot-marinaded Carrots and Turnips
(for 4–6 portions)

$^3/_4$ lb carrots
$^1/_4$ lb turnips
Master Sauce
2 tablespoons chopped
   parsley

3 tablespoons butter
2 tablespoons sherry

Dice the carrots and turnips and simmer them in the Master
Sauce. Drain thoroughly. Heat the butter in a frying-pan on a
low heat. Add the carrots and turnips. Turn the vegetables in
the butter for 2 minutes. Add the sherry and continue to turn
and stir gently for 1 more minute. Sprinkle with parsley and
serve.

### Hot-marinaded Celery Stir-fried with Chinese Dried Mushrooms
(for 4–5 portions)

1 lb celery
4 oz Chinese dried
   mushrooms
$^1/_2$ tablespoon cornflour
   blended with 2 tablespoons
   Vegetable Broth

3 tablespoons butter
1 tablespoon sherry
$^1/_4$ teaspoon vegetable
   bouillon powder
Master Sauce

Clean the celery thoroughly. Slice diagonally into 2-inch long pieces. Soak the mushrooms in hot water for $1/2$ an hour and remove the stems. Slice the mushrooms into thin strips, retaining 3–4 tablespoons of mushroom water. Blend the mushroom water with the cornflour mixture, vegetable bouillon powder and sherry.

Bring the Master Sauce to the boil and simmer the celery in it for 10 minutes. Remove and drain. Heat the butter in a frying-pan on a medium heat. Add the mushrooms to stir-fry for 2 minutes. Add the hot-marinaded celery. Stir-fry them together on a high heat for 2 minutes. Pour in the cornflour mixture blended with mushroom water, etc. Turn and stir a few times, and serve as soon as the gravy has thickened.

### Hot-marinaded Deep-fried Aubergine (or Asparagus Tips) with Transparent Noodles and Sliced Cucumber
(for 4–6 portions)

$3/4$ lb aubergine (or asparagus tips)
Master Sauce
oil for deep-frying
3 oz transparent noodles (before soaking)
4-inch segment of cucumber
4 tablespoons butter
$1/2$ cup Vegetable Broth

$1/2$ teaspoon salt
$1/3$ teaspoon vegetable bouillon powder
1 tablespoon light soya sauce
2 teaspoons sesame oil
1 tablespoon chopped watercress

Cut the aubergine into $1/2$-inch-thick slices. Scrape the cucumber segment, cut into two, and further slice into matchstick strips. Soak the noodles in warm water for $1/4$ of an hour and drain.

Simmer the aubergine in the Master Sauce for 10 minutes, and drain. Deep-fry in the oil for 3 minutes and drain. Heat the butter in a large frying-pan. When melted, add the cucumber and stir-fry on a medium heat for 1 minute. Add the noodles. Turn them together on a low heat for 2 minutes. Add the salt, vegetable bouillon powder and soya sauce. Pour in the Vegetable Broth. Allow to cook over a medium heat for 2 minutes. Add the deep-fried aubergine. Turn the pieces over among the noodles and cucumber a few times. Sprinkle with sesame oil and chopped watercress and serve in a large bowl.

In this dish the hot-marinaded, deep-fried aubergine, or asparagus tips, provides a richness which is counterbalanced by the freshness of the cress and cucumber.

### Hot-marinaded Deep-fried Vegetable Steak with Stir-fried Spinach
(for 4–5 portions)

| | |
|---|---|
| 3 pieces bean-curd (tofu) cake or about ¹/₂lb | 2 tablespoons butter |
| ³/₄ lb spinach | 2 tablespoons soya sauce |
| 2 cloves garlic | 4 tablespoons Vegetable Broth |
| 2 slices ginger root | 2 tablespoons sherry |
| 2 tablespoons vegetable oil | Master Sauce |

Cut each 'steak' into 4–6 pieces or into chips. Wash and dry the spinach thoroughly, and remove some of the tougher stems. Crush the garlic and shred the ginger.

Simmer the pieces of 'steak' in Master Sauce for 10 minutes. Deep-fry in hot oil for 3 minutes. Drain and keep hot. Heat the vegetable oil in a large frying-pan or saucepan. Add the garlic and ginger. Stir-fry on a high heat for ¹/₂ a minute. Add the spinach and butter. Stir-fry them in the oil for 3 minutes. Add the soya sauce and sherry. Continue to stir-fry over high heat for 2 minutes. Lift the spinach on to a serving dish with a perforated spoon. Place the 'steaks' on top of the spinach. Add the Vegetable Broth to the frying-pan, stir and pour the 'gravy' in the frying-pan over the 'steaks'.

## Mixed-fried Hot-marinaded Vegetables with Hot Peanut Butter Sauce
(for 4–6 portions)

The people from Fukien Province like to use sesame paste or Hot Peanut Butter Sauce in their stir-fry cooking, in both meat and vegetable dishes. This is one of their more aromatic vegetable dishes.

| | |
|---|---|
| $^1/_2$ lb broccoli | 2 cloves garlic |
| $^1/_2$ lb asparagus tips | 1 slice ginger root |
| $^1/_2$ lb carrots (young) or courgettes | 4 tablespoons Hot Peanut Butter Sauce (see page 84) |
| Master Sauce | 2 tablespoons sherry |
| oil for deep-frying | 2 tablespoons sesame oil |

Break the broccoli into 2–3-inch pieces (reject the coarser stems). Cut the asparagus into 2–3-inch segments. Scrape the carrots or courgettes and cut diagonally into 1–2-inch segments. Crush the garlic.

Simmer the carrots or courgettes in the Master Sauce for 20 minutes; add the asparagus and broccoli and simmer for another 10 minutes. Strain. Heat the sesame oil in a frying-pan. Add the ginger and garlic. Stir-fry on a medium heat for $^1/_2$ a minute. Add the vegetables and Peanut Butter Sauce, and stir-fry them together for $1^1/_2$ minutes. Add the sherry. Continue to stir-fry for $^1/_2$ a minute, then serve.

## Hot-marinaded Bean-Curd Sticks with Quick-fried Bean Sprouts
(for 5–6 portions)

Bean-curd sticks are dried skin of bean curd. They are cream coloured with an enamel-like surface.

| | |
|---|---|
| 6 oz bean-curd sticks | 1 teaspoon bean-curd (tofu) cheese |
| Master Sauce | |

<sup>3</sup>/<sub>4</sub> lb bean sprouts
<sup>1</sup>/<sub>2</sub> teaspoon salt
1 tablespoon soya sauce
1 tablespoon hoisin sauce

3 tablespoons Vegetable
 Broth
2 stalks spring onion
4 tablespoons vegetable oil

Soak the bean-curd sticks in warm water for 2 hours. Cut into 2–3-inch segments. Chop the spring onion finely.

Simmer the bean-curd sticks in the Master Sauce for 30 minutes, and drain. Heat 3 tablespoons of oil in a large saucepan on a high heat. Add the bean sprouts, sprinkle with salt, and stir-fry quickly for 2 minutes. Add the remaining oil to the middle of the pan by scooping and pushing the bean sprouts to the sides. Add soya sauce, hoisin sauce and tofu cheese to the oil. Mix quickly with the oil. Add the Vegetable Broth. As it boils rapidly, stir and turn the sprouts. Add the bean-curd sticks. Stir-fry them together with the bean sprouts for 2 minutes. Turn on to a serving dish. Sprinkle with chopped spring onion and serve.


### Hot-marinaded Cabbage with Sweet and Sour Sauce
(for 4–6 portions)

1<sup>1</sup>/<sub>2</sub> lb cabbage (Savoy)
Master Sauce
1 teaspoon salt

4 tablespoons vegetable oil
<sup>1</sup>/<sub>2</sub> cup Sweet and Sour Sauce
 (see page 81)

Cut the cabbage against the stem into 1<sup>1</sup>/<sub>2</sub>-inch slices. Simmer them in Master Sauce for 7–8 minutes and drain. Heat the oil in a large frying-pan. When hot, add the cabbage, sprinkle with salt and stir-fry on a high heat for 3 minutes. Pour in the Sweet and Sour Sauce. Stir and blend gently. Serve as soon as the sauce thickens and becomes translucent.

## *Hot-marinaded Shredded Carrots with Shredded Radish and Hot-Pickled Szechuan Cabbage*
(for 4–6 portions)

1 lb carrots
4 oz radishes
Master Sauce
2 oz hot-pickled Szechuan
  cabbage (canned)
3 tablespoons Vegetable
  Broth

3 tablespoons vegetable oil
1 tablespoon sesame oil
1 tablespoon chopped
  coriander leaves

Top and tail the carrots and radishes, then scrape and clean them. Slice into 2–3-inch-long strips about $1/4$-inch wide. Cut the Szechuan cabbage into similar-size pieces.

Simmer the carrots in the Master Sauce for 15 minutes and drain. Heat the oil in a large frying-pan. When hot, add the radish and Szechuan cabbage, and stir-fry together on a high heat for 2 minutes. Add the carrots and stir-fry them together for 3 minutes. Add the sesame oil and Vegetable Broth and stir-fry for a further 3 minutes. Sprinkle with chopped coriander and serve.

# Boiling and Stewing

## RED-COOKING, WHITE-COOKING, HOT-ASSEMBLY AND CLEAR-SIMMERING

Boiling is not frequently used as a method of cooking vegetables in China, except for parboiling, which is intended purely for tenderizing hard vegetables. Even then, vegetables can be equally well tenderized through sautéing, braising, deep-frying or slow cooking in broth, etc., without losing much of their flavour through dispersing their already high water content in the even greater quantity of water in which they are boiled. To add water to water, or to cook water in water, is hardly an acceptable method of cooking, and yet it is the one most universally used in this country!

Parboiling is, however, often used in Chinese cooking, mainly because stir-frying, the most frequently used method of cooking employed in China, is often a very short process – a question of a minute or two, or sometimes less – and some pre-tenderizing of food is often necessary to keep up with the rapid pace of flavouring and tenderizing during the final stage of cooking. Much of parboiling in China is in fact done in broth, so that as the foods or vegetables are tenderized their flavours are also intensified. Usually no great quantity of broth is required. The vegetables do not have to be 'drowned'; they have only to be turned in broth, with the broth reducing all the while. When the broth reduces during cooking, and when more and other types of food are added to the pot, we come to a situation which is pretty near to stewing. When the pre-cooked materials, which have been cooked and prepared in

59

different ways, whether by deep-frying, parboiling, braising, etc., are assembled together in a short process of stewing, we have what we call 'Hui' or 'Hot-assembly'.

Chinese 'stewing' is precisely the same as the Western method, except in Chinese 'stewing' we usually add some soya sauce, or soya paste, or both and chopped or shredded ginger, and sugar to enhance flavour (apart from the other normal seasonings). In 'Hot-assembly' at least one ingredient has been deep-fried beforehand, usually cut tofu cakes, and very often a drop or two of sesame oil is added for that earthy aromatic effect at the last moment of cooking. As is the nature of stews, they are seldom 'pure' dishes where only one vegetable is cooked in the pot; more generally they are an assembly of several vegetables and other ingredients, conforming with the Chinese concept of the 'orchestration of flavours'. However, there are a number of cases where vegetables are prepared and cooked on their own which are extremely successful and easily achieved.

## RED-COOKED VEGETABLES

Typical of these are the so-called 'red-cooked' (which simply means cooked with soya sauce, or stewed with soya sauce) dishes. Indeed, almost any food can be red-cooked with success.

### Red-cooked Aubergines
(for 4–6 portions)

$1^1/_2$ lb aubergines  
$^1/_2$ lb medium-size tomatoes  
3 tablespoons vegetable oil  
1 tablespoon butter  
2 cloves garlic  

$^1/_2$ cup Vegetable Broth  
3 tablespoons red wine  
$^1/_2$ teaspoon vegetable bouillon powder  
1 teaspoon sugar

2 slices ginger root        1$^{1}/_{2}$ teaspoons sesame oil
$^{1}/_{2}$ teaspoon salt            pepper (to taste)
3 tablespoons soya sauce

Cut the aubergines into 2$^{1}/_{2}$ by 1$^{1}/_{2}$-inch pieces. Skin the tomatoes and cut into quarters. Crush the garlic and shred the ginger.

Heat the oil in a casserole. Add the garlic and ginger, and stir-fry for $^{1}/_{2}$ a minute. Add the aubergines and turn the pieces in the oil for 2 minutes on a high heat. Add the tomatoes. Sprinkle the contents with salt, sugar, soya sauce, vegetable bouillon powder and finally pour in the broth. Turn the contents over a couple of times. Reduce the heat to low, cover, and cook for 15 minutes. Open the lid. Add the butter, pepper, wine and sesame oil. Turn the contents gently and cook for a further 5 minutes. Serve.

For non-vegetarians, omit the salt and add $^{1}/_{2}$–1 chicken stock cube, 4–5 tablespoons of meat gravy – from red-cooked meat – and 1 tablespoon of dried shrimps at the beginning of the stewing. Use chicken broth or good meat stock instead of Vegetable Broth in the cooking.

## Red-cooked Broccoli (or Brussels Sprouts)
### (for 4–6 portions)

Broccoli and Brussels sprouts can be prepared in precisely the same manner as the aubergines in the previous recipe, except the cooking times can be reduced from 15 minutes to 10 minutes, and the tomato can be omitted. The broccoli should be broken into individual branches (about 2 inches long), and the sprouts should each be cut in four, before they are fried.

For non-vegetarians, use good meat stock or chicken broth instead of Vegetable Broth, add a few tablespoons of red-cooked meat gravy, and $^{1}/_{2}$–1 chicken stock cube. These should enhance the 'meaty' flavour of the vegetables considerably.

## Red-cooked Cabbage (or Celery)
### (for 4–6 portions)

One of the most popular and successful of red-cooked vegetables. Indeed it is so well liked that even meat eaters sometimes choose it in preference to meat dishes. It is prepared and
cooked in much the same way as the previous red-cooked
vegetables. As it is a Chinese 'classic', apart from being a very
useful dish in any context, it is justifiable to spell out all the
details again.

$1^1/_2$–2 lb cabbage (crinkly
  Savoy rather than hard; or
  Chinese cabbage)
3 tablespoons vegetable oil
2 tablespoons butter
2–3 tablespoons red wine (or
  sherry)
1–2 cloves garlic
1 medium onion

1–2 slices ginger root
  (optional)
4 tablespoons soya sauce
$^1/_2$ teaspoon salt
$^1/_2$ teaspoon vegetable
  bouillon powder
1 teaspoon sugar
$^1/_2$ cup Vegetable Broth
pepper (to taste)

Crush the garlic, shred the ginger, and cut the onion into thin
slices. Cut the cabbage into 1-inch-thick strips. Remove the
root and cut each strip into quarters.

Heat the oil and melt the butter in a heavy saucepan or
casserole. Add the garlic, ginger and onion, and stir-fry for 1
minute. Add the cabbage and turn it in the oil for 2 minutes
until it is completely covered. Add all the other ingredients.
Turn the contents over a few times. Reduce the heat as low as
possible, cover and leave to cook for 10–12 minutes. Pour in
the wine or sherry. Turn the contents over a couple of times
and serve.

For non-vegetarians, omit the salt and add $^1/_2$–1 chicken
stock cube, 3–4 tablespoons of red-cooked meat gravy and 2
teaspoons of dried shrimps at the beginning of the stewing.

use chicken broth or good meat stock instead of Vegetable Broth.

Celery can be red-cooked in the same manner as cabbage, and with equal success. The same applies to celeriac or red cabbage. But cauliflower is usually 'white-cooked' rather than red-cooked, which means it is cooked in a white broth rather than with soya sauce.

## Red-cooked Carrots (and/or Turnips)

Carrots can be red-cooked in the same manner as any of the previous vegetables, but they require much longer cooking – 30–40 minutes – as do turnips cooked in the same manner. The important point about cooking these two vegetables is that after the initial stir-frying on a high heat, they should be covered and simmered over very low heat for the rest of the cooking. Turn the vegetables over once every 15–20 minutes to ensure even cooking. Or they can be cooked in a casserole placed in an oven at about 150°C (300°F) mark 2 for 1 hour.

For non-vegetarians, omit the salt and add $1/2$–1 chicken stock cube, 3–4 tablespoons of red-cooked meat gravy and 2 teaspoons of dried shrimps at the stewing stage. Use chicken broth or good meat stock instead of Vegetable Broth.

When carrots and turnips are cooked in this manner, they should be cut in triangular wedges (about $1^1/_2$ inches). Since they require about the same length of time in cooking, they can mix in the same pot, thus providing some contrast in colour, texture and taste.

For non-vegetarians, the favourite meat cooked with turnips in China is beef. Hence the best meat gravy to use would be red-cooked beef gravy and beef stock cube, in addition to the other ingredients.

### Red-cooked Dried Beans (Haricot or Butter Beans) and Chestnuts

All these items can be red-cooked, but they are seldom served on their own. Dried beans must be soaked overnight, and both dried beans and chestnuts need to be parboiled for 20 minutes before being added to red-cook with the other items. They may be added to carrots and turnips, but much more often chestnuts are cooked together with red-cooked meat (pork or beef). Beans of this type which require the longest cooking ($1^1/_2$ hours upwards) are usually fried in oil and put into the pot first before all the other ingredients. These latter may be tofu cakes (quickly deep-fried), transparent pea-starch noodles, and a host of other vegetables, which require no more than a few minutes or 10–12 minutes to cook, such as mushrooms, peas, cauliflower, leeks, etc. The beans are simply red-cooked first and made ready, whilst the other items are being prepared; they are then all assembled to cook together. Here we approach the 'assembled' dishes, where small amounts of tofu cheese and sesame oil are often added to enhance flavour and aroma.

## WHITE-COOKED VEGETABLES

As previously mentioned, 'white-cooking' simply means cooking without the use of soya sauce, or soya paste. Because these last two soya bean products are used universally as the general flavourer in Chinese cooking, their significance and importance cannot be over-estimated. Once they are omitted, a sort of 'vacuum' is created, which has to be filled. In non-vegetarian cooking, this vacuum is filled in by the use of concentrated chicken broth or meat stock, supplemented by such items as dried prawns, dried mussels and oysters, shrimp sauce, vegetable bouillon powder, etc.

In vegetarian cooking, the gap is largely bridged by the use of stronger vegetarian broth (by simmering a greater quantity of dried beans in preparing the broth), light soya sauce supplemented by the use of tofu cheese, vegetable bouillon powder, dried light-coloured mushrooms, manufactured mushroom sauce and items (tofu and the like) which have been deep-fried for a short period in sesame oil, or items with specific flavours, such as lily-bud stems, as well as all the pickled and salted items. The stronger spices, such as pepper, curry, chilli and mustard, are also more frequently employed than in non-vegetarian cooking. In the West milk and cream can also be used with success.

One of the most commonly seen white-cooked dishes is:

### White-cooked Cabbage
(for 6–8 portions)

$1^1/_2$–2 lb cabbage
3 tablespoons vegetable oil
2 tablespoons butter
2 tablespoons white wine
2 teaspoons sesame oil
pepper (to taste)
$^1/_4$ pint enriched Vegetable Broth (made from $2^1/_2$ lb dried beans)
1–2 cloves garlic

1–2 slices ginger root
1 medium-size onion
$^1/_2$ teaspoon salt
2 tablespoons light soya sauce
$^3/_4$ teaspoon vegetable bouillon powder
1 tablespoon bean-curd (tofu) cheese
4 tablespoons top of milk
1 teaspoon sugar

Crush the garlic, shred the ginger and slice the onion very thinly. Cut the cabbage into $^1/_2$-inch-thick slices.

Prepare the enriched Vegetable Broth, by soaking $2^1/_2$ lb of dried beans overnight, then simmering them very slowly in 3 pints of water in a covered saucepan for 3–$3^1/_2$ hours, or cooking them in a casserole in the oven at about 150–170°C

(300–325° F) mark 2–3 for 3 hours. The resultant reduced liquid is added to ordinary Vegetable Broth. The same result can be achieved using a pressure-cooker, in 30–35 minutes. Forty per cent bean-water is added to 60 per cent broth.

Heat the oil in a saucepan, add garlic, ginger and onion, and stir-fry them together on a medium heat for 1 minute. Add the cabbage and butter, and turn the vegetables until all the butter has melted and the vegetable pieces are coated with oil. Add the salt, sugar, tofu cheese, vegetable bouillon powder, light soya sauce, enriched 'broth' and top of the milk. Turn the contents several times, cover and cook gently for 12–15 minutes. Open the lid, add the wine and sesame oil, and sprinkle the contents with freshly ground pepper. Turn the vegetables over a couple of times and serve.

For non-vegetarians, simply use chicken broth instead of Vegetable Broth, and a chicken stock cube instead of salt.

### White-cooked Celery
(for 4–6 portions)

Repeat the previous recipe, using celery instead of cabbage. For smaller amounts of celery reduce the quantities of the various ingredients in proportion.

### White-cooked Cauliflower

Cauliflower can be white-cooked and treated in precisely the same manner as celery and cabbage in the previous recipes, except that a white Fu-Yung Sauce (see page 82) is often poured over the cauliflower just before serving. As the cauliflower will break into unsightly pieces if stirred around with too great vigour (unlike cabbage and celery which can be roughly treated without any ill effect), it is often better undercooked, say, for only 5–6 minutes, and then steamed for another 3–4 minutes in a heatproof dish in which it has been carefully arranged, with the white Fu-Yung Sauce carefully poured over the vegetable.

White-cooking is applicable to a majority of vegetables which only require cooking for between 10 and 20 minutes. It can, therefore, be used with good effect with broccoli, Brussels sprouts, French beans, cabbage, courgettes, marrows, etc., but is not often used with aubergines (which have too red a colour and are more suitable red-cooked) or with such vegetables as carrots, turnips, chestnuts, which require a good deal longer cooking, and are therefore also best red-cooked. It is never used with quick-cooked leaf vegetables, such as spinach, bean sprouts, lettuce, watercress, etc., or with sliced cucumber, as they are best stir-fried in oil or butter, with as little liquid as possible added so that they maintain their crisp, crunchy quality when served. Any cooking in liquid will cause them to wilt.

### *White-cooked Broccoli (or Brussels Sprouts, French Beans, Courgettes, Marrow, etc.)*

All these vegetables can be white-cooked in the same manner as cauliflower: that is, stir-fried for a short period and cooked for 5–6 minutes under cover along with the same ingredients as cabbage or cauliflower. Marrow and courgettes must of course be cut into suitable slices or wedges first. Like cauliflower, they are often best steamed for 3–4 minutes, with Fu-Yung Sauce poured over them just before serving. These last touches enhance the tenderness and colour of the vegetables. Sometimes pickled or salted vegetables, such as Red-in-Snow (well-known Chinese salted pickled greens), are finely chopped and sprinkled over the plain white-cooked vegetables to give them added interest.

## *White-cooked Bamboo-shoots with Chinese Mushrooms*
### (for 4–6 portions)

1 can bamboo-shoots (8–10 oz)
3–4 oz Chinese dried mushrooms (before soaking)
2 oz green peas
2 tablespoons vegetable oil
1½ tablespoons butter
1 tablespoon white wine (or sherry)
1 teaspoon sesame oil

1 clove garlic
1 slice ginger root
2 tablespoons light soya sauce
¾ tablespoon bean-curd (tofu) cheese
½ teaspoon vegetable bouillon powder
½ cup enriched Vegetable Broth (see page 65)

Crush the garlic and shred the ginger. Cut the bamboo-shoots into ½-inch wedges. Soak the mushrooms in a bowlful of hot water for ½ an hour. Discard the water and stems, and cut each mushroom into quarters.

Heat the oil in a heavy saucepan (or casserole). Add the garlic and ginger and stir-fry on a medium heat for ½ a minute. Add the bamboo-shoots. Continue to stir-fry for 2–3 minutes. Add the soya sauce, tofu cheese, vegetable bouillon powder and enriched Vegetable Broth. Cover and cook on a low heat for 15 minutes. Add the butter, mushrooms and peas. Turn the contents over 3–4 times and continue to cook on a low heat for 5 minutes. Add the wine and sesame oil. Stir the contents around a few times and serve.

## HOT-ASSEMBLY

In this form of 'stewing', a good many types of vegetable, many prepared in different ways, are assembled together in one pot, and cooked for a short while before serving (usually in a large bowl or tureen, or in the cooking pot or casserole itself). In the marrying of one material with another, this is a similar process to stir-frying, but while in stir-frying the materials are fried together, in 'hot-assembly' the materials are cooked or stewed together for a short period. Two of the most universally used materials for hot-assembly are bean-curd (tofu) cakes and transparent pea-starch noodles: because they absorb a great deal of gravy (or soup) in the dish as well as the flavours of all the other ingredients they add coherence to a dish apparently composed of many items thrown together, as well as providing added substance.

### The 'Lo-Han Dish of the Monks' Mixed Vegetables'
(for 6–10 portions)

2 bean-curd (tofu) cakes
4 oz transparent pea-starch noodles (before soaking)
3 oz dried bamboo-shoots
3 oz Chinese dried mushrooms
1/2 lb broccoli
1/2 lb cabbage
1 oz 'wood ears' fungi
1/4 lb celery
2 cloves garlic
1 medium onion
1/2 teaspoon salt
2 1/2 tablespoons soya sauce

1/2 tablespoon tofu cheese
1/2 teaspoon vegetable bouillon powder
1 teaspoon sugar
1 1/2 cups Vegetable Broth
3 tablespoons butter
1/4 lb aubergine
2 stalks 'golden noodles' (lily bud stems)
1/4 lb French beans
oil for deep-frying
2 teaspoons sesame oil
2 tablespoons dry sherry
pepper (to taste)

Cut each piece of tofu cake into 8 pieces. Deep-fry them for 3 minutes and drain. Soak the noodles in water for 5 minutes and drain. Soak the mushrooms in 1 cup of warm water for 1/2 an hour. Remove the stalks and cut each mushroom into quarters (retain the water). Soak the 'wood ears' in warm water for 1/2 an hour and rinse to clean. Soak the dried bamboo-shoots and 'golden noodles' for $^1/_2$ an hour and cut into 1-inch sections (discard water).

Prepare the vegetables by slicing the cabbage into $^1/_2$-inch slices and breaking the broccoli into 1-inch branches. Cut the celery and beans into $1-1^1/_2$-inch-long sections and the aubergines into $^1/_2$-inch-thick slices. Crush the garlic and cut the onion into thin slices.

Heat 2 tablespoons of oil in a casserole. Add the onion and garlic and stir-fry on a high heat for 1 minute. Add all the vegetables and butter and stir-fry them together for 3–4 minutes. Add the salt, soya sauce, tofu cheese, vegetable bouillon powder, sugar, pepper and Vegetable Broth and mushroom water. Bring to the boil and simmer them over a low heat for 15 minutes. Add the tofu and transparent noodles. Turn them in the soup and vegetables. Allow the contents to heat together for a further 7–8 minutes. Pour in the sherry and sprinkle with sesame oil. Serve in the casserole itself or in a large tureen.

For non-vegetarians, repeat the previous recipe and toss in $^1/_2-^3/_4$ lb of red-cooked meat (pork or beef) together with a few tablespoons of gravy to cook with the vegetables during their stewing. The resulting stew of meat and vegetables is quite irresistible. Not infrequently a whole knuckle-end of pork is red-cooked for $1^1/_2-2$ hours, then added to a pot of Lo-Han Dish of Mixed Vegetables and simmered together for 15–20 minutes before serving.

### Hot-assembly of Shredded Bamboo-shoots and Bean-Curd with Strips of Cucumber and Chinese Mushrooms
(for 6–8 portions)

| | |
|---|---|
| 1 can of bamboo-shoots (8–10 oz) | 2 teaspoons sesame oil |
| | 1 clove garlic |
| 3 oz dried bamboo-shoots | 1 slice ginger root |
| 1 cake tofu (bean-curd) | 3 stalks spring onion |
| oil for deep-frying | 2 tablespoons oil |

4-inch segment of a medium-
   size cucumber
3 oz dried Chinese
   mushrooms
$^1/_2$ cup bean broth (cook
   beans in pressure-cooker
   for 30–35 minutes with
   twice their weight of water)
2 tablespoons white wine (or
   sherry)

$^1/_2$ teaspoon salt
$1^1/_2$ tablespoons light soya
   sauce
$^1/_2$ tablespoon tofu cheese
$^1/_2$ teaspoon vegetable
   bouillon powder
2 tablespoons butter

Shred the bamboo-shoots into $1^1/_2$–2-inch-long and $^1/_4$-inch-
thick strips. Soak the dried bamboo-shoots for $^1/_2$ an hour and
shred in the same way. Chop the tofu and unpeeled cucumber
to same size. Soak the dried mushrooms for $^1/_2$ an hour,
remove the stems and cut into similar strips. Crush the garlic,
shred the ginger, and cut the spring onion into $1^1/_2$-inch pieces.

Deep-fry the tofu strips and dried bamboo-shoots for 2–3
minutes and drain. Heat the oil in a saucepan or frying-pan
with lid. Add the ginger, garlic and half the spring onion. Stir-
fry for $^1/_2$ a minute, add the two types of bamboo-shoots and
continue to stir-fry for 3 minutes. Add the salt, soya sauce, tofu
cheese, vegetable bouillon powder and 'bean broth'. Stir once,
cover and leave to cook for 5–6 minutes. Add the butter, tofu,
mushrooms, the rest of the spring onion and the cucumber
strips. Stir and toss until the 5 types of 'strip' are well inter-
woven. Leave to cook for 3 minutes. Sprinkle with wine and
sesame oil. Toss and serve.

### Hot-assembly of Chestnuts, Sliced Lotus Root, Gingko Nuts, Peanuts, Chinese Mushrooms and Bean-Curd
(for 6–8 portions)

$^1/_2$ lb peeled chestnuts
$^1/_4$ lb gingko nuts

$^1/_2$ tablespoon tofu cheese
$^1/_2$ teaspoon vegetable

<sup></sup>

| | |
|---|---|
| $^{1}/_{4}$ lb peanuts | bouillon powder |
| 3 oz green peas | 2 tablespoons butter |
| $^{1}/_{4}$ lb dried lotus root | 1 cake tofu (bean-curd) |
| 3 oz Chinese dried | vegetable oil for deep-frying |
| mushrooms | $^{1}/_{2}$ cup Vegetable Broth |
| 3 tablespoons vegetable oil | 2 teaspoons sesame oil |
| 2 tablespoons soya sauce | |

Soak the lotus root in water for 1 hour and the mushrooms for $^{1}/_{2}$ an hour. Remove stalks from mushrooms. Cut the tofu into 8 pieces and the lotus root into $^{1}/_{4}$-inch slices. Deep-fry lotus root and tofu for 3 minutes and drain. Parboil the chestnuts, peanuts, and gingko nuts for 15 minutes and drain away water.

Heat the oil in a casserole. Add all the nuts and stir-fry together for 3 minutes. Add the lotus root, mushrooms, tofu pieces, butter and all the other ingredients. Turn them around until well mixed. Place the casserole in a preheated oven to cook at 170°C (325°F) mark 3 for 35 minutes. Sprinkle with sesame oil and serve.


# CLEAR-SIMMERING

'Clear-simmering' differs from hot-assembly in that the cooking is much longer, and in order to maintain the clarity of the soup, which should be like a clear consommé, cooking is usually at a low temperature – about 140–150°C (275–300°F) mark 1–2 in the oven – for quite a time. Because of the 'static' cooking, every piece of vegetable retains its clear-cut, native state and colour. To prepare a first-class clear-simmered dish the broth in which the vegetables are cooked has to be specially prepared. This is generally done by simmering those various roots and stems of vegetables which do not produce any cloudiness in the liquid in water for $1^{1}/_{2}$–2 hours, and filtering them twice through triple layers of cheesecloth. The preparation and cutting (or even carving) of the vegetables is done with great care, then they are parboiled for about a couple of minutes before being placed in the broth for the final cooking. The final dish derives its flavour from three sources: the broth, the first lot of vegetables which are simmered in the broth for a long time, and the final lot of vegetables which are only simmered in the broth for a short period. These last provide the freshening effect. The majority of clear-simmered dishes are 'semi-soup' dishes, always welcomed by rice-eaters. The clear broth required for such a purpose can generally be prepared as follows:

## Clear Broth for Clear-simmering

$^1/_2$ lb cabbage stems
$^1/_2$ lb stem of spring greens
  (or broccoli)
$^1/_4$ lb turnips
$^1/_4$ lb potato
$^1/_4$ lb dried beans

$^1/_4$ lb runner beans
$^1/_4$ lb carrots
3 pints water
$1^1/_2$ teaspoons salt
1 tablespoon light soya sauce

Clean the vegetables thoroughly, cut into approximately $1^1/_2$-inch-square pieces. Place in a casserole and add the water and seasonings. Cover and simmer for 3 hours at 150°C (300°F) mark 2 for 1 hour, and 140°C (275°F) mark 1 for 2 hours. Strain twice through triple layers of cheesecloth. Almost any vegetable or dried vegetable can be cooked in this broth. But for the best results, usually only one vegetable is used as the main ingredient, and small amounts of other vegetables or dried vegetables are used as supplementary ingredients.

## Clear-simmered Chinese Cabbage (or ordinary Cabbage, or Celery, or Broccoli)
### (for 4–6 portions)

$^1/_2$ lb stem and root of
  cabbage
$1^1/_2$ lb Chinese cabbage
2 oz Chinese dried
  mushrooms
1 pint Clear-simmer Broth

$^1/_2$ tablespoon butter
1 teaspoon salt
1 tablespoon light soya sauce
pepper (to taste)
$^1/_2$ teaspoon vegetable
  bouillon powder

Clean the stem and root of the cabbage very thoroughly. Cut into $1^1/_2$-inch pieces. Parboil for 5–6 minutes and discard the water. Soak the mushrooms in hot water for $^1/_2$ an hour, remove the stems and cut into quarters (discard water). Slice the cabbage into $1$–$1^1/_2$-inch slices.

Place the stem and root of the cabbage at the bottom of a casserole. Pour in the broth. Bring to the boil and simmer gently in the oven at 150°C (300°F) mark 2 for $^1/_2$ an hour. Add the cabbage leaves, mushrooms, and all the other ingredients and continue to simmer for $^1/_2$ an hour at the same temperature. Turn the cabbage. Reduce to 140°C (275°F) mark 1 and continue to simmer for a further $^1/_4$ of an hour. The cabbage is ready to serve in the casserole; adjust seasoning, if necessary. The great appeal of this dish lies in the sweetness and clarity of flavour of the principal vegetable.

## Clear-simmered Marrow or Sprouts or Runner Beans
### (for 4–6 portions)

2 lb young large marrow (or
  courgettes)
$^1/_4$ lb cucumber
1 oz Chinese dried
  mushrooms and/or 1 oz

$^1/_2$ tablespoon butter
1 teaspoon salt
1 tablespoon light soya sauce
$^1/_4$ teaspoon vegetable
  bouillon powder

Chinese dried bamboo-          pepper (to taste)
   shoots
1¹/₂ pints Clear-simmer Broth

Clean and scrape the skin of the marrow, removing all the hard
outer skin. Cut into 2–3-inch pieces. Cut the cucumber into 1-
inch sections and then slice vertically into ¹/₆-inch-thick slices,
each piece to include skin. Soak the mushrooms and dried
bamboo-shoots in warm water for ¹/₂ an hour. Remove the
stems from the mushrooms; cut them into quarters and the
bamboo-shoots into strips; discard water.

Place the bamboo-shoots and mushrooms at the bottom of a
casserole, pour in the broth and add the marrow and butter.
Sprinkle with seasonings and flavourers. Place the casserole in
the oven at 150°C (300°F) mark 2 to simmer for ¹/₂ an hour.
Add the cucumber and continue to simmer for another ¹/₂ an
hour at 140°C (275°F) mark 1. Serve in the casserole. (If sprouts
or runner beans are used they should first be parboiled for 3–4
minutes and drained before being placed in the pot.)

### Clear-simmered Asparagus
(for 4–6 portions)

1¹/₂ lb asparagus                1 teaspoon salt
1 oz Chinese dried              1 tablespoon light soya sauce
   mushrooms and/or 1 oz        ¹/₂ teaspoon vegetable
   dried bamboo-shoots             bouillon powder
1 pint Clear-simmer Broth       pepper (to taste)
¹/₂ tablespoon butter

Scrape the stem end of the asparagus until quite clean. Cut
each piece of asparagus into two sections (the tip section and
harder root-stem section). Parboil the root sections for 5–6
minutes and discard the water.

Soak the mushrooms and dried bamboo-shoots in warm

water for $^1/_2$ an hour. Remove the stems from the mushrooms. Cut each one into quarters and the bamboo-shoots into strips.

Place the tougher ends of the asparagus, the bamboo-shoots and the mushrooms at the bottom of the casserole. Simmer them at 150°C (300°F) mark 2 in the oven for $^1/_2$ an hour. Add the asparagus tips and butter, and all the seasonings and flavourers, and simmer for a further $^1/_2$ an hour at 140°C (275°F) mark 1. Serve.

With the Chinese propensity for cross-cooking, we naturally wander into cooking mixed pots of vegetables, although, as already mentioned, clear-simmering is generally used to bring out the flavour of the one main vegetable. When several vegetables are cooked together, the two types of ingredient which are often cooked with them are transparent pea-starch noodles and tofu cakes. These two items can be used singly or together. Being neutral in flavour themselves, they have the great advantage of absorbing and retaining the flavours of the other ingredients, apart from providing a meat-like body to the dish.

### Clear-simmered Mixed Vegetables
(for 6–8 portions)

| | |
|---|---|
| $^1/_2$ lb cabbage | 3 oz Cos lettuce |
| $^1/_4$ lb sprouts | 1 tablespoon chopped chives |
| $^1/_4$ lb marrow | 1 teaspoon salt |
| $^1/_4$ lb broccoli | $1^1/_2$ tablespoons light soya |
| $^1/_4$ lb carrots | sauce |
| 4 oz transparent pea-starch | $^1/_4$ teaspoon vegetable |
| noodles (before soaking) | bouillon powder |
| $1^1/_2$ pints Clear-simmer Broth | pepper (to taste) |
| 2 oz watercress | |

Clean the vegetables thoroughly, discarding all the unappealing leaves and roots. Cut the cabbage into 1-inch slices, the sprouts into halves or quarters, the broccoli into individual branches and carrots slantwise into 1-inch-long wedges. Chop the lettuce at $1\frac{1}{2}$-inch intervals and cress into 1-inch segments. Scrape and clean the skin of the marrow and cut into $1\frac{1}{2}$-inch pieces. Parboil the cabbage, sprouts, broccoli and carrots for 3 minutes and drain. Soak the noodles in water for 10 minutes and drain.

Place the cabbage, sprouts, marrow, broccoli and carrots at the bottom of a casserole. Add the broth, salt, soya sauce, vegetable bouillon powder and pepper. Bring to a gentle boil, and place in the oven at 140°C (275°F) mark 1 for $\frac{1}{2}$ an hour. Add the cress, lettuce and chives, and the transparent noodles. Simmer for another 20 minutes, and serve in the casserole.

For non-vegetarians, simply add chicken broth to the broth for clear-simmering on a 50–50 basis, and in addition parboil 1 heaped tablespoon of dried shrimps and add them to simmer with the other vegetables from the beginning.

## Clear-simmered Mixed Vegetables with Vegetable Roots

To Westerners, vegetable roots may convey something coarse, but by the Chinese they are sometimes regarded as delicacies, if prepared with care, and are extremely appealing especially when served from the kitchens of vegetarian Buddhist monasteries.

Repeat the previous recipe. Use $\frac{3}{4}$ lb of specially selected large stems or roots of cabbage, broccoli, greens. Clean thoroughly, and cut or carve them carefully into oblong pieces (approximately $1 \times \frac{1}{2} \times \frac{1}{4}$ inch) discarding anything or any part which is unappealing or imperfect. Parboil them for 5 minutes and drain. Simmer them very gently in Clear-simmer Broth for $\frac{1}{2}$ an hour at 150°C (300°F) mark 2 and add them, together with the additional broth, to the other vegetables. Simmer for 1 hour at 140°C (275°F) mark 1. The resultant carved pieces of vegetables are picked out with chopsticks and consumed with relish by connoisseurs when the dish arrives on the table.

### Clear-simmered Vegetables with Dried and Pickled Vegetables

Sometimes vegetable dishes are enriched by the addition of dried and pickled vegetables, which naturally have a much more concentrated flavour than fresh vegetables. These are added in small quantities (1–3 oz) to the simmering. In order that they do not over-colour the broth in the dish, they are generally soaked first, then drained and parboiled for a minute or two before being added to the main mixed stock. The most frequently used dried vegetables are of course mushrooms and dried lily bud stems ('golden needles'); the latter has a distinctive marshy taste with which the Chinese are familiar, but it may not seem so appealing to the Westerner, and can therefore be omitted. Pickles are often simply minced coarsely and a tablespoon or two scattered over the cooked dish before serving. 'Wood ear' is a variety of fungus which is used frequently in Chinese cooking; it has little flavour of its own, but is added for its crunchy texture and colour contrast (it is generally black).

# Sauces for Vegetables

As a rule we Chinese do not go in for made-up sauces, preferring to wait for the 'sauces' to come out of the food as it is being cooked, to which a few basic flavourers and seasonings are added: Vegetable Broth, soya sauce, hoisin sauce, sugar, vegetable bouillon powder, vinegar and wine. For non-vegetarian dishes, the basic liquid flavourers are usually concentrated chicken broth, which can be produced by adding chicken stock cubes to ordinary chicken broth, shrimp sauce, oyster sauce, or meat gravy, from red-cooking. The addition of these meaty ingredients, or meat essence, to vegetables turns Chinese vegetable dishes almost into meat dishes and is the reason for their popularity with savoury-lovers throughout the world. However, Chinese vegetable cooking does use a few very popular made-up sauces, which can easily be added to most vegetable dishes, especially those which are stir-fried, or stir-fried and braised.

### *Hot Black Beans and Tomato Sauce (or Ratatouille Chinoise)*
#### (for 5–6 portions)

$^1/_2$ tablespoon salted black beans

$^1/_2$ tablespoon yellow bean paste

2 slices ginger root

1 medium-size onion

2 cloves garlic

1 red chilli pepper

1 tablespoon soya sauce

2 medium courgettes

4 small aubergines

$^1/_2$ tablespoon hoisin sauce

$^3/_4$ cup Vegetable Broth

$^1/_2$ teaspoon vegetable bouillon powder

$^1/_4$ cup red wine

| 4 medium-size tomatoes | 2 teaspoons sugar |
| 4 tablespoons vegetable oil | 1 tablespoon sesame oil |

Soak the black beans in water for $^1/_2$ an hour and drain. Chop the onion and pepper into very small pieces, removing seeds. Crush the garlic and ginger. Skin the tomatoes and cut each into four. Dice the aubergines and courgettes into $^1/_2$-inch cubes.

Heat the oil in a heavy pan. When hot add the black beans, pepper, onion, garlic, ginger. Stir-fry for 2 minutes over a medium heat. Add the tomatoes, aubergines, courgettes and soya paste, and continue to stir-fry gently for 5 minutes. Add the Vegetable Broth. Stir and leave to simmer for 20 minutes. Add the wine, sugar, soya sauce, hoisin sauce and vegetable bouillon powder. Stir and continue to simmer for about 20 minutes or until the liquid begins to thicken. Add sesame oil. Stir a few more times, and the 'ratatouille chinoise' is ready. A few tablespoons of this 'ratatouille' makes a welcome addition to the majority of stir-fried dishes, vegetarian or semi-veg-etarian, or it can be added to boiled rice at the table. The following are some of the stir-fried, or stir-braised dishes to which a few tablespoonfuls of Hot Black Beans and Tomato Sauce ('ratatouille chinoise') can be added:

Plain Stir-fried Spinach
Plain Stir-fried Bean Sprouts
Plain Stir-fried Young Leeks
Plain Stir-fried Celery
Plain Stir-fried Chinese Cabbage
Stir-fried and Braised Broccoli and Cauliflower
Stir-fried and Braised Brussels Sprouts

This sauce, here adapted for Western use, originates from the west Chinese province of Szechuan.

## Sweet and Sour Sauce
(for 4–6 portions)

This well-known Chinese sauce can be added to many vegetable as well as meat dishes.

3 tablespoons tomato purée
2 tablespoons soya sauce
2½ tablespoons sugar
3 tablespoons vinegar
2–3 tablespoons fruit juice (orange, pineapple, apple, etc.)
¾ tablespoon cornflour (blended in 4 tablespoons water)

2 tablespoons sherry
1 tablespoon chopped mixed pickles
1 tablespoon vegetable oil
4 tablespoons water

Mix the first seven ingredients in a bowl and stir until they are well blended. Stir-fry the pickles in oil for ½ a minute. Pour in the water. When it starts to boil vigorously pour in the blended sauce mixture. Stir until the mixture thickens and is translucent.

Food which has been stir-fried can be cooked for a short time in this sauce and then served, or the sauce can be poured over foods on their serving dishes. If this sauce is used, enough of it should be added to cover all the foods on the serving dish (not just a couple of tablespoons).

The following are a few of the many dishes to which it can be added:

Plain Stir-fried Bean Sprouts
Plain Stir-fried Celery
Plain Stir-fried Tomato and Cucumber
Plain Stir-fried Chinese Cabbage
Plain Stir-fried and Braised Broccoli or Cauliflower
Plain Stir-fried and Braised Aubergines (or Courgettes or Marrows)

## Mushroom Sauce
(for 5–6 portions)

<sup>3</sup>/<sub>4</sub> lb mushrooms
6 large Chinese dried
  mushrooms
1 cup Vegetable Broth
1 tablespoon soya sauce
<sup>1</sup>/<sub>2</sub> tablespoon cornflour
  (blended in 4 tablespoons
  water)

1 tablespoon sherry
1 oz butter
1<sup>1</sup>/<sub>2</sub> tablespoons vegetable oil
<sup>1</sup>/<sub>2</sub> tablespoon hoisin sauce
<sup>1</sup>/<sub>2</sub> teaspoon vegetable
  bouillon powder
1<sup>1</sup>/<sub>2</sub> teaspoons sesame oil

Clean the mushrooms and cut into thin slices. Soak the dried mushrooms in <sup>3</sup>/<sub>4</sub> of a cup of hot water for <sup>1</sup>/<sub>2</sub> an hour. Discard the stalks and cut the mushrooms into thin strips. Retain the mushroom water.

Heat the butter in a saucepan. When hot, add the sliced fresh mushrooms and sauté and stir-fry gently for 5–6 minutes. Sauté the strips of dried mushrooms in oil for 5–6 minutes. Combine the mushrooms in one pan, and stir them together for 1 minute. Pour in the Vegetable Broth, add mushroom water, soya sauce, hoisin sauce and vegetable bouillon powder. Allow the contents to simmer gently for 15 minutes over a low heat, stirring occasionally. Add the cornflour mixture, sesame oil and sherry. Stir until the mixture thickens. The sauce is usually poured directly on to rice, or fried rice, and is a very useful addition when few savoury dishes are available.

## Fu-Yung Sauce
(for 4–5 portions)

The Chinese Fu-Yung Sauce is a white sauce made with egg white (and for non-vegetarians, usually with minced chicken). Vegetarians can make it by simply combining seasoned beaten egg white with a roux made from flour, butter and milk.

| 4 egg whites | salt, pepper (to taste) |
| 3 tablespoons butter | $^{1}/_{2}$ teaspoon vegetable |
| 2 tablespoons plain flour | bouillon powder |
| $^{1}/_{4}$ pint top of milk | |

Beat the egg white with a rotary beater for 15–20 seconds or until it becomes slightly stiff. Make a roux by stirring flour into hot butter in a saucepan and gradually adding milk. Finally, stir in the egg white to blend with the roux, add the vegetable bouillon powder and season with salt and pepper. (Cream is optional but 2–3 tablespoons can be added here.) Fu-Yung Sauce can be added to most light-coloured vegetable dishes in which not too much soya sauce or soya paste have been used. Its whiteness makes it a suitable sauce to apply to green vegetables, such as broccoli, cauliflower, cucumber, sprouts, peas and leeks, particularly when the vegetables have not been cooked in dark-coloured sauces; it gives the greenness of the vegetable a more glistening and jade-like appearance.

### Five Willow Sauce
(for 4–6 portions)

This is a sharp vinegary sauce, normally used by non-vegetarians on fish. But for vegetarians who like the sharp taste of vinegar it can be served with other dishes.

| 1 medium-size green pepper | $^{3}/_{4}$ cup water |
| 3 oz bamboo-shoots | 3 tablespoons sugar |
| 3 oz carrots | 4 tablespoons vinegar |
| 2 red chilli peppers | 1 tablespoon cornflour |
| 2 tomatoes | 1 tablespoon sherry |
| $^{1}/_{2}$ cup mixed pickles | 2 tablespoons soya sauce |

Shred the pepper, chilli peppers, bamboo-shoots and carrots into matchstick strips. Skin and cut the tomatoes into quarters, which are then quartered again.

Bring $1/2$ a cup of water to boil in a saucepan. Add the sugar and soya sauce. Blend the cornflour, sherry and vinegar in the rest of the cup of water. When well blended pour into the pan. Stir until the liquid thickens. Add the shredded peppers, bamboo-shoots, carrots, tomato and pickles. Allow them to simmer gently in the pan for 4–5 minutes. Stir a couple of times and serve in a bowl or sauceboat. The sauce is hot, sharp and has a strong tang. It can be added to anything which has a milder taste, e.g. omelette, bean sprouts, salads and fish.

### *Hot Peanut Butter Sauce*
(for 5–6 portions)

In the Fukien province of China this sauce is usually made with sesame paste (tahini). Peanut butter blended with sesame oil can be used as an alternative.

3 tablespoons peanut butter
2 tablespoons sesame oil
2 tablespoons soya sauce
2 tablespoons sherry
2 teaspoons sugar
3 tablespoons Vegetable
  Broth

1 tablespoon hoisin sauce
2 tablespoons tomato purée
1 teaspoon chilli sauce (or $1/2$
  teaspoon Chinese chilli
  oil)

Heat the ingredients together gently for 3 minutes over a low heat, stirring continuously. This is a Southern sauce, often poured over cooked tofu, well-cooked hard vegetables, or over noodles and pastas.

# Soups

The principal function of Chinese soups is to provide a savoury liquid to swallow when eating quantities of rice and other foods, and to give a balance to the variety of dishes on the table. They are meant to be taken throughout the meal and not just as first courses. There can therefore be more than one soup served at a meal, placed on the table along with all the other dishes. During a Chinese banquet the soups often mark the beginnings and ends of different series of dishes.

For full flavour, a Chinese soup is usually made in four stages: (a) preparation of the basic broth; (b) the addition of dried, salted or pickled ingredients to give added flavour or piquancy; (c) the cooking of the principal ingredients in the broth, either long/slow-cooking or instantly; (d) the addition of 'freshening', or aromatic or quickly cooked ingredients towards the last stage of the cooking.

Naturally not all soups are prepared by going through all four stages. Because a great variety of materials can be used and cross-blended in the different stages, the number of soups which can be produced, as with most varieties of Chinese dishes, is again only a question of permutation.

First of all let us start with the preparation of the basic broth. In non-vegetarian cooking, basic broth is produced by simmering together chicken, pork and bone for a long period of time, and if a 'freshener' is required some freshly minced chicken meat is usually added for a few minutes cooking before it is strained. The result is an extremely tasty and flavoursome broth, which can be combined with a vast variety of ingredients into a first-class soup within a very short time. In order to produce a tasty and flavoursome vegetarian soup, after the production of the basic broth, greater care has to be exercised in the selection of the principal ingredients and greater attention is also paid to the selection of dried, pickled and salted materials for flavouring, as well as to the 'fresheners' added during the last stages of the cooking. In the modern kitchen some concessions should be made to Western materials, such as yeast extract and Marmite, which will help to make the soup savoury, especially in darker ones. With lighter coloured soups, or white soups, greater reliance has to be placed on vegetable bouillon powder.

## BASIC VEGETABLE BROTH

Basic Vegetable Broth is prepared in China by the double process of long-simmering and short-cooking: long-simmering of 2–3 vegetables, including dried beans (for 2–2$^1/_2$ hours), followed by short-cooking in the same liquid of 1–2 soft vegetables (for 10–15 minutes). The liquid is then strained to provide the broth. More elaborately, Basic Vegetable Broth is produced by simmering together 1 unit of mushroom stalk, $^1/_2$ unit of dried mushroom, $^1/_2$ unit of peanuts, 1$^1/_2$ units of yellow beans, or any type of dried beans, together with 1 unit of any two or three types of vegetable, such as carrot, turnip, lentils, swedes, marrow, parsnips, celery, potato, onions, cauliflower, cabbage, etc., with 5–6 units of water for 2 hours. The vegetables are then strained and the broth seasoned with soya sauce, salt and pepper, vegetable bouillon powder and yeast extract. If $^1/_2$ lb amounts of vegetables are used, 3$^1/_2$–4 pints of water will be needed for simmering to produce sufficient soup for 4–6 portions. In the case of dark-coloured soup, 1$^1/_2$ tablespoons of soya sauce, $^1/_2$ teaspoon of salt and 1 teaspoon of yeast extract (or Marmite) should be added for seasoning. For white soups, 1 teaspoon of salt and 1 teaspoon of vegetable bouillon powder should be added as basic seasoning. For soups of one particular flavouring, such as onion, celery, mushroom, carrot, etc., a bias of $^1/_2$–1 extra unit of that vegetable can be added together with $^1/_2$ pint of extra water. This basic broth, white or dark, is used for preparing all soups. With a quantity in hand, many Chinese soups can be produced almost instantly. If a non-vegetarian broth is wanted, simply add 1 chicken stock cube and $^1/_4$ pint of water to the above version of Basic Vegetable Broth.

### Simplified Vegetable Broth

Make up $1^1/_2$ lb of vegetables with any three (or all) of the following vegetables: cabbage, carrots, cauliflower, tomato, onion, turnip, leeks, broccoli, Brussels sprouts, runner beans, French beans, marrows. Add to them 8 oz of mushroom stalks. Bring them to the boil in $2^1/_2$ pints of water, and simmer very gently for 1 hour. Add $1^3/_4$ tablespoons of soya sauce and 1 teaspoon of vegetable bouillon powder (or if non-vegetarian, chicken stock cube) and simmer for another 10 minutes. Strain for use as broth or stock. It is a good idea to make more broth than needed for immediate use, then to freeze the rest in ice-cube trays or other small containers.

## QUICK-COOK SOUPS – SOUPS PREPARED FROM VEGETABLES WHICH REQUIRE VERY LITTLE COOKING

### Strips of Cucumber Soup
(for 4–5 portions)

| | |
|---|---|
| 6-in piece of cucumber | 1 teaspoon sesame oil |
| 2 pints Basic Vegetable Broth (dark or white) | 1 tablespoon soya sauce |

1 heaped tablespoon Chinese
  dried mushrooms (or
  other dried mushrooms)

$^1/_4$ teaspoon vegetable
  bouillon powder
salt and pepper (if required)

Soak the mushrooms in $^1/_2$ cup of hot water for $^1/_2$ an hour, removing stalks, if any, and add to the broth.

Scrape away the soft centre of the cucumber, after cutting the cucumber into 3 equal pieces. Cut the skin and firm outside rim of the cucumber vertically into thin strips 2 inches long and $^1/_4$ inch wide.

Heat the broth in a saucepan, adding soya sauce and vegetable bouillon powder and simmer for 1 minute. Add the cucumber strips. Simmer for 3–4 minutes. Adjust for seasoning, sprinkle with sesame oil and serve in a tureen or in individual bowls.

### *Spinach Soup*
(for 4–5 portions)

$^1/_2$ lb best leaf spinach
1 clove garlic (crushed)
1 tablespoon butter
1 tablespoon soya sauce
1 teaspoon vegetable
  bouillon powder
$^1/_2$ tablespoon vegetable oil

2 pints dark Basic Vegetable
  Broth
1 heaped tablespoon Chinese
  dried mushrooms (or
  other dried mushrooms)
1 teaspoon sesame oil
salt and pepper (if required)

Soak the mushrooms in $^1/_2$ cup of hot water for $^1/_2$ an hour removing stalks, if any, and add to broth. Remove any stalk or unsightly spinach leaves.

Bring the broth to boil and leave to simmer for 1 minute. Heat butter and oil in a large saucepan. Add garlic and mushrooms and stir-fry for $^1/_2$ a minute. Add the spinach and stir-fry on a high heat for 1 minute. Pour in the broth, add the soya sauce and leave to simmer for 5 minutes. Adjust for seasonings, sprinkle with sesame oil and serve in a tureen.

## Green Jade Soup (or Cream of Spinach Soup)
### (for 5–6 portions)

$^1/_2$ lb chopped or minced
  spinach
$^1/_2$ small can creamed
  sweetcorn
$1^1/_2$ pints Basic Vegetable
  Broth (white or dark)
$1^1/_2$ tablespoons butter

1 tablespoon soya sauce
2 teaspoons vegetable
  bouillon powder
$^1/_2$ tablespoon cornflour
  (blended with 2
  tablespoons water)
salt and pepper (to taste)

Thaw the spinach if frozen. Mix the creamed sweetcorn with the broth and heat together to a simmer. Stir the cornflour into the mixture to thicken it.

Heat the butter in a large saucepan. When melted, stir in the spinach. Stir-fry for 2 minutes and pour in the creamed corn and broth mixture. Add the soya sauce and vegetable bouillon powder. Stir until the spinach is well blended into the liquid. Adjust for seasoning. Simmer for 2 minutes and serve. Add more butter if wanted richer.

All Chinese Quick-cook Soups can be prepared in the same manner as Cucumber Strip Soup and Spinach Soup with only minor variations: often more shredded dried mushrooms are added to enhance the taste where the flavour of mushroom does not conflict with the flavour of the main vegetable used in the soup, or one other ingredient, such as 'egg-flower' (beaten egg dripped slowly into the soup) or transparent noodle is added to provide contrast or variation in colour, texture or substance, or a small quantity of chopped salted or pickled vegetable is added to give an additional tang or piquancy.

## Tomato Soup
### (for 5–6 portions)

| | |
|---|---|
| 4–5 medium-size tomatoes | 2 teaspoons vegetable |
| 1 egg | bouillon powder |
| 2$^1$/$_2$ pints Basic Vegetable | 1$^1$/$_2$ teaspoons sesame oil |
| Broth (dark) | 1 tablespoon dry sherry |
| 2 stalks spring onion | pepper (to taste) |
| 1 tablespoon soya sauce | |

Finely chop the spring onion. Cut each tomato into six. Beat the egg lightly with a fork.

Heat the broth in a saucepan. Lower the heat immediately as it starts to boil. Add the tomato and allow to simmer for 5 minutes. Add the soya sauce and vegetable bouillon powder. Stream the beaten egg into the soup along the prongs of a fork, in as thin a stream as possible, allowing it to trail over the soup. Pepper the soup liberally; adjust for seasoning. Add the sesame oil and sherry. Sprinkle with spring onion and serve.

## Mushroom Soup
### (for 5–6 portions)

| | |
|---|---|
| 8 medium-size mushrooms | 2 tablespoons butter |
| 4 medium-size Chinese dried | 1$^1$/$_2$ tablespoons soya sauce |
| mushrooms (or any dried | 2 teaspoons vegetable |
| mushrooms) | bouillon powder |
| 2$^1$/$_2$ pints Basic Vegetable | 2 tablespoons sherry |
| Broth (dark) | pepper and salt (to taste) |

Soak the dried mushrooms in $^1$/$_2$ cup of hot water for $^1$/$_2$ an hour. Discard the stems and slice into thin strips. Remove the stems of the fresh mushrooms and slice each mushroom into 8–10 thin slices.

Heat the broth in a saucepan, adding the soaked dried

mushrooms. Add the soya sauce and vegetable bouillon powder. Heat the butter in another saucepan. Add the sliced fresh mushrooms. Turn over in the butter a few times and allow to sauté for 3 minutes. Pour into the broth and dried mushrooms in the first pan and simmer for 3 minutes. Pour in the sherry, adjust for seasoning and serve.

## Watercress Soup

Watercress Soup can be quickly prepared in the same manner as Spinach Soup or Strips of Cucumber Soup, simply by substituting watercress for spinach or cucumber. The main point is to wash the cress thoroughly and remove some of the muddier roots. One tablespoon or two of chopped Chinese pickled greens (such as Red-in-Snow) may be added to provide extra tang and flavour.

## Celery Soup

Celery Soup can be prepared in the same way as Spinach Soup and Cucumber Soup, except that the celery, sliced diagonally into $^2/_3$-inch segments, should be simmered in the broth for a longer period: 8–10 minutes. Generally a couple of extra tablespoons of Chinese dried mushrooms are used to enhance the flavour, as celery, being a somewhat stronger flavoured vegetable, is able to counterbalance the stronger taste of mushrooms in the broth.

## Leek Soup

Leek Soup can be prepared in the same manner as Celery Soup, and both require about the same length of cooking. For $2–2^1/_2$ pints of Leek Soup, 2–3 oz of transparent pea-starch noodles are often added. They should be soaked in warm water for a couple of minutes before being added to the broth to simmer with the leeks. As pea-starch noodles do not become soft and mushy in cooking, they provide an interesting mixture of taste and texture alongside the dried mushrooms.

## Lettuce Soup

Lettuce Soup can be prepared in precisely the same manner as Cucumber Soup. Both vegetables require the minimum length of cooking. Indeed such soups should always be freshly made and drunk immediately they are prepared, so that the vegetables do not become limp. In making the soup choose the crispiest lettuce, and cut the leaves into $1/4$-inch-wide strips. Always use the white rather than the dark-coloured Basic Vegetable Broth. To enhance the flavour, a large pinch of finely chopped chives or spring onion may be sprinkled over the soup before serving, or a small quantity of watercress (about $1/4$ the quantity of lettuce) may be added to simmer together with the lettuce.

## Egg-Flower Soup

Egg-Flower Soup is one of the commonest soups served in China. It sometimes consists of no more than boiling water to which is added a couple of tablespoons of soya sauce and $1/2$ teaspoon of vegetable bouillon powder. This is poured into a large soup bowl and lightly beaten egg is trailed into the soup by pouring it in a very thin stream along the prongs of a fork. The liquid should not be stirred until the egg has coagulated into flowerets. More flavour is provided by sprinkling a large pinch ($1/4$-$1/2$ tablespoon) of finely chopped chives or spring onion over the soup along with a teaspoon of sesame oil. The soup will of course be much tastier if the Basic Vegetable Broth (white) is used instead of just boiling water. Occasionally a teaspoon or two of vinegar may be added to give the soup and additional tang.

# LONGER COOKED SOUPS

Because the majority of Chinese soups are clear soups it is essential to cook them slowly, apart from instant soups. It is a good idea to prepare Chinese soups in a casserole in the oven, where the heating is usually more even and easily controlled.

### *Hot Cabbage Soup*
(for 6–8 portions)

Hot Cabbage Soup can be white or dark, simply by varying the broth used. For darker soup, soya sauce is added.

1 medium-size cabbage
3 pints Vegetable Broth
3 tablespoons Chinese dried mushrooms
1 red chilli pepper
1¹/₂ tablespoons vegetable oil or butter

salt or pepper (to taste)
3 teaspoons vegetable bouillon powder or soya sauce

Soak the dried mushrooms in ¹/₂ a cup of hot water for ¹/₂ an hour. Remove the stems and slice the mushrooms into thin strips. Cut the pepper into 6–8 strips and remove the pips. Remove the stem from the heart of the cabbage, and slice it into 6–8 thin slices. Cut the cabbage leaves into ¹/₂-inch wide slices.

Heat oil or butter in a casserole. Add the pepper and turn the strips in the oil for ¹/₂ a minute. Add the cabbage stem slices, turn them in the oil for 1 minute and leave to sauté gently for 3 minutes. Add the cabbage leaves and pour in the broth. Bring to the boil and place in a casserole to simmer gently in the oven for ¹/₂ an hour at 170°C (325° F) mark 3. Add the mushroom strips. Adjust for seasoning (add soya sauce for a dark soup or salt, vegetable bouillon powder and pepper for a white one) and simmer again for a further 10–15 minutes at the same temperature. Serve in a large bowl or tureen, or in individual bowls.

### Heart of Spring Greens or Cabbage Soup
(for 5–6 portions)

| | |
|---|---|
| 1½ lb spring greens (about 4 plants) or cabbage | 1 tablespoon soya sauce |
| 2½ pints Basic Vegetable Broth | 2 teaspoons vegetable bouillon powder |
| 2 heaped tablespoons dried Chinese mushrooms (or other types of dried mushroom) | 2 tablespoons butter |
| | 2 tablespoons dry sherry |
| | salt and pepper (to taste) |

Remove the outer leaves of the spring greens or cabbage for use in some other dish. Cut each heart vertically into quarters. Soak the mushrooms in ½ cup of hot water for ½ an hour and remove the stalks.

Heat the butter in a casserole. When it has melted turn the mushrooms and heart of greens in it for 2 minutes. Pour in the broth and add the soya sauce and vegetable bouillon powder. Bring to the boil and place the casserole in a preheated oven at 170°C (325°F) mark 3 for ¾ of an hour. Add sherry and adjust for seasoning.

The soup can be served either in the casserole or in individual bowls. One of the attractions of this soup is that the heart of greens or cabbage become extremely tender, yet still retain their neat original shape.

### Turnip Soup

Turnips are used in soups far more frequently in China than in the West. Non-vegetarians usually cook them with beef broth, or other strong-tasting meat, such as mutton, while vegetarians often use a slightly stronger Basic Vegetable Broth by adding 3–4 tablespoons of dried mushrooms instead of mushroom, and 2 slices of ginger root. It is cooked in exactly the same way as the Heart of Spring Greens Soup in the previous recipe, except that it is simmered for $1\frac{1}{4}$–$1\frac{1}{2}$ hours in a casserole in the oven at 170°C (325°F) mark 3. To serve 5–6 persons use about $\frac{3}{4}$ to 1 lb of turnips, sliced diagonally into $\frac{1}{2}$-inch pieces, to $2\frac{1}{2}$ pints of strengthened broth.

### *Asparagus and Bamboo-shoot Soup*
(for 6–8 portions)

1 lb fresh asparagus
$\frac{1}{4}$ lb bamboo-shoots (canned)
3 oz dried bamboo-shoots
3 pints Basic Vegetable Broth
1 tablespoon soya sauce
2 teaspoons vegetable bouillon powder

$\frac{1}{4}$ teaspoon yeast extract
$1\frac{1}{2}$ tablespoons vegetable oil
2 tablespoons sherry
salt and pepper
1 teaspoon sesame oil

Remove the tough parts of the roots of asparagus. Slice the remainder diagonally into $1\frac{1}{2}$-inch segments. Cut the bamboo-shoots to approximately the same size segments. Soak the dried bamboo-shoots in hot water for $\frac{1}{2}$ an hour and slice into thin strips.

Heat the oil in a casserole. Add the dried bamboo-shoot strips and stir-fry for 2 minutes. Pour in the broth, add the asparagus, bamboo-shoots, soya sauce, vegetable bouillon powder and yeast extract. Bring to the boil and place the casserole in a preheated oven for 1 hour at 170°C (325°F) mark 3. Remove the casserole from the oven. Add the sherry and sesame oil, adjust for seasoning and serve.

## Brussels Sprouts Soup
(for 4–6 portions)

$^3/_4$ lb Brussels sprouts
3 oz dried bamboo-shoots
1 oz hot-pickled Szechuan
  cabbage
$2^1/_2$ pints Basic Vegetable
  Broth

2 tablespoons butter
$1^1/_2$ tablespoons soya sauce
1 teaspoon vegetable
  bouillon powder
$^1/_2$ teaspoon yeast extract
salt and pepper

Clean the sprouts and remove any unsightly outer leaves. Cut each sprout into quarters. Soak the dried bamboo-shoots in 1 cup of hot water for $^1/_2$ an hour. Slice into thin 1-inch strips. Slice the Szechuan cabbage into thin pieces.

Heat the butter in a casserole. When melted, add the Szechuan cabbage and dried bamboo-shoots, and stir-fry for 2 minutes. Add the broth and sprouts, soya sauce, vegetable bouillon powder and yeast extract. Bring to the boil, and place the casserole in a preheated oven at 150°C (300°F) mark 2 for 1 hour. Adjust for seasoning and serve.

## Broccoli Soup
(for 4–5 portions)

Broccoli Soup can be prepared in precisely the same manner as the Brussels Sprouts Soup of the previous recipe, simply by using broccoli instead of Brussels sprouts, cutting the former into small individual branches. A small quantity of transparent pea-starch noodles may be added to give variety to the texture.

## Mixed Vegetable Soup
(for 5–6 portions)

2 medium-size onions
3 oz water chestnuts

2 heaped tablespoons dried
  mushrooms

1½ tablespoons cornflour
(blended in ½ pint milk)
2½ pints Basic Vegetable
Broth (light)
3 oz carrots
3 oz bamboo-shoots
3 oz French beans
1 teaspoon salt
3 oz cabbage
3 oz celery
½ teaspoon yeast extract
2 oz transparent pea-starch
noodles
2 tablespoons butter
2 teaspoons vegetable
bouillon powder
salt and pepper (to taste)

Cut all the vegetables diagonally into ½-inch-thick slices or segments. Soak the dried mushrooms in 1 cup of hot water for ½ an hour. Remove stalks if necessary. Slice into thin slices.

Heat the butter in a casserole. Add the dried bamboo-shoots and stir-fry for 2 minutes. Add all the other vegetables and stir-fry for 3–4 minutes. Pour in the broth, add the noodles, salt, yeast extract, vegetable bouillon powder and pepper to taste. Bring to the boil, and place the casserole in a preheated oven at 150°C (300°F) mark 2 for 1 hour. Adjust for seasoning. Thicken with a milk/cornflour mixture, if desired.

## Chinese Onion Soup
### (for 4–6 portions)

8 medium-size onions
2 heaped tablespoons dried
Chinese mushrooms
2½ pints Basic Vegetable
Broth
3 tablespoons watercress
(chopped)
2 tablespoons butter
1 tablespoon vegetable oil
1 tablespoon cornflour
(blended in 4 tablespoons
water)
2 tablespoons soya sauce
2 teaspoons vegetable
bouillon powder
½ teaspoon yeast extract
salt and pepper

Slice 6 onions into thin slices and keep in one heap. Slice the other 2 onions and keep in a separate heap. Soak the mushrooms in $^1/_2$ cup of hot water for $^1/_2$ an hour and slice into thin slices, discarding the stalks.

Heat the butter in a casserole. Stir-fry the larger heap of onion in the butter for 3 minutes. Pour in the broth and add the mushrooms, soya sauce, vegetable bouillon powder and yeast extract. When the contents start to boil place the casserole in a preheated oven at 170°C (325°F) mark 3 for 1 hour and 20 minutes. Stir the contents once every 20 minutes. After 1 hour, add the blended cornflour to thicken.

Whilst the casserole is cooking in the oven, heat the oil in a small frying-pan, and stir-fry the smaller heap of onion gently for 4–5 minutes until slightly brown. When the contents of the casserole are about ready, place the frying-pan of onion under the grill to toast the onion until it is quite crispy. Mix this onion with chopped watercress and use the mixture to garnish the soup, which is served either in the casserole or a large tureen, or in individual bowls.

## THICK SOUPS

Although most Chinese soups are clear, there are a number of thick soups. They are usually prepared with tofu (bean-curd), peas, long-cooked rice, and egg whites (Fu-Yung). Some of them are 'sweet' soups, taken as refreshments at teatime (and indeed they are very refreshing and sustaining at that time of the day as I have lately experienced after strenuous tennis!) or used as a kind of punctuation between a long series of savoury dishes during party dinners. Let us start with a couple of them:

## Sweet Rice Congee
(for 5–6 portions)

Sweet Rice Congee is the Chinese version of rice pudding, except it is prepared without using milk or cream.

| | |
|---|---|
| $^1/_2$-$^3/_4$ cup pudding rice | peanuts, chow chow |
| $^1/_4$ cup red beans | (sugared ginger) etc. |
| 3 pints water | 4–5 tablespoons sugar |
| 1 cup (approx.) mixed glacé | 1 tablespoon honey |
| fruit and nuts, including | |
| dates, lotus seeds (when | |
| available), almonds, | |

Wash the rice and place in a heavy pan with the red beans. Add the water and bring to the boil. Reduce heat to minimum. Stir the contents every $^1/_4$ of an hour. After $^3/_4$ of an hour pour in the nuts and fruit. Continue to simmer gently and stir every 20 minutes or so for a further hour. Stir in the sugar and honey, blend them well and serve.

In the Western kitchen a simplified version of this recipe can be prepared by heating a cupful of dried fruit and nuts in $^1/_2$ pint of milk for 10–15 minutes with the addition of 2 tablespoons of sugar and then stirring in a tin of rice pudding. But we Chinese feel that the Sweet Rice is more refreshing without milk or cream.

## Sweet Peanut Soup
(for 4–5 portions)

| | |
|---|---|
| 2 cups peanuts (raw, | 1 tablespoon cornflour |
| unroasted) | (blended in 4 tablespoons |
| 2 pints water | water) |
| 4–5 tablespoons brown sugar | 1 teaspoon baking soda |
| 1 tablespoon honey | |

Heat the water in a heavy pan. Stir in the baking soda. When it boils add the peanuts. Lower the heat to minimum. Stir the contents every $^1/_4$ of an hour and continue to heat for $1^1/_2$ hours. Add cornflour to thicken. Stir in the sugar and honey. Blend well and serve.

## Sweet Pea Soup

Repeat the preceding recipe using dried split peas instead of peanuts, but the peas will first have to be soaked overnight and then simmered for $1^1/_2$–2 hours. The soup should be filtered through a fine sieve before adding cornflour, sugar and honey, then reheated for 1 minute and served. This is a refreshing soup which provides a sustaining snack at any time of the day.

## Green and White Soup
(for 5–6 portions)

### GREEN PORTION

$^1/_2$ lb chopped or minced spinach

2 cups Basic Vegetable Broth (dark)

$^1/_2$ teaspoon salt

$1^1/_2$ teaspoons sugar

2 teaspoons vegetable bouillon powder

$1^1/_2$ tablespoons cornflour (blended in 6 tablespoons water)

$1^1/_2$ tablespoons butter

### WHITE PORTION

4 egg whites

$^1/_2$ cup milk

$^1/_4$ cup cream

1 cup Basic Vegetable Broth (light)

1 tablespoon cornflour (blended in 3 tablespoons water)

1 teaspoon salt

$^1/_2$ teaspoon vegetable bouillon powder

Beat the egg white with a rotary beater for $^1/_4$ of a minute. Add all the other ingredients for the *White portion* and blend well.

Heat the butter in a saucepan. When it has melted, pour in the spinach and turn it in the butter for 1 minute. Pour in the 2 cups of broth. When hot, add all the other ingredients for the *Green portion*. Stir until the liquid begins to boil and thickens. Allow to simmer gently for 2–3 minutes.

See that all the ingredients for the *White portion* are well blended and pour into a saucepan. Heat until the liquid begins to boil and thicken.

Pour the green soup into a large soup bowl or tureen, and pour the white soup into the centre of the green soup, taking care not to mix the two. Ladle out and serve in individual bowls.

## Green Pea Soup
(for 4–6 portions)

| | |
|---|---|
| $^2/_3$ lb of green peas | 1 teaspoon salt |
| $1^1/_2$ pints Basic Vegetable Broth (light) | $1^1/_2$ tablespoons cornflour (blended in 6 tablespoons water) |
| 2 tablespoons butter | $^1/_2$ pint milk |
| 2 teaspoons vegetable bouillon powder | |

Add the peas to 1 pint of boiling water. Heat for 20 minutes. Drain and mash in an electric blender until smooth and creamy.

Heat the butter in a saucepan. Add the peas. Turn and blend with the butter. Pour in the broth. When hot, add all the other ingredients. Stir until the liquid begins to boil and thicken. Heat gently for another 3 minutes and serve.

## Red Bean Congee ('Soft Rice')
(for 4–6 portions)

This is a sweet soup, with a porridge-like consistency, usually eaten on its own as a snack.

$^1/_4$ lb rice (Patna or any kind of long-grained rice) and 2 $^1/_2$ pints water
$^1/_2$ lb red beans and 2 pints water

4–6 tablespoons sugar (or to taste)

Wash the rice and place in a heavy pan with 2$^1/_2$ pints of water. Bring to the boil, then simmer very gently for 1$^1/_2$ hours.

Place the red beans in another saucepan with 2 pints of water. Bring to the boil and simmer very gently for 1$^1/_2$ hours.

Combine the red beans with the rice. Stir and blend them well, and continue to heat very gently for another $^3/_4$ of an hour, stirring every 10 minutes. Add sugar and serve in individual bowls. Excellent served at teatime, to supplement tea and cakes, especially on a cold wintry day.

## Basic Bean-Curd Soup
(for 5–6 portions)

2 cakes tofu (bean-curd)
2 pints Basic Vegetable Broth
1 teaspoon salt
2 teaspoons vegetable bouillon powder

1 tablespoon soya sauce
1 teaspoon tofu cheese
1 tablespoon cornflour (blended in 3 tablespoons water)

Cut the tofu cakes into $^1/_2$–1-inch cubes.

Heat the broth in a saucepan. Add the salt, vegetable bouillon powder, soya sauce and tofu cheese. Blend well and add the cornflour, blended in water. Stir until the soup thickens slightly. Add the bean-curd. Heat through (3–4 minutes) and serve.

## Enriched Bean-Curd Soup

Enriched Bean-Curd (Tofu) Soup can be produced by simmering a number of additional ingredients in the previous soup before adding the tofu; for example, diced mushrooms (4 large dried mushrooms, first soaked in hot water for $1/2$ an hour and diced into $1/6$–$1/4$-inch-square pieces), spring onion (2 stalks chopped into $1/4$-inch segments), lily bud stalks (chopped into $1/4$-inch segments after 1 hour's soaking in hot water), $1/4$ cup of green peas. After these additional ingredients have been simmered for $1/2$ an hour, add 1 salted duck's egg (chopped), 1 tablespoon of butter, and stir in $1/2$ cup of double cream. Finally add the tofu. When the latter has heated through (3–4 minutes), the soup will be ready to serve.

## Hot and Sour Soup

The well-known Hot and Sour Soup in an extension of the Enriched Bean-Curd Soup. It is made simply by blending 2 tablespoons of vinegar, 2 tablespoons of soya sauce, $1/2$ teaspoon of black pepper (or to taste) and $1^1/2$ tablespoons of cornflour in 6 tablespoons of Basic Vegetable Broth. Stir this mixture into the Enriched Bean-Curd Soup, which must be hot. When the soup is further thickened, beat an egg lightly, and trail it into the soup very slowly, along the prongs of a fork, in as thin a stream as possible. After about 10 seconds the egg will have coagulated and formed into 'egg-flower'. Give the soup a stir and serve.

For non-vegetarians, a few tablespoons of chopped prawn or chicken may be added to the broth before it thickens.

## Fu-Yung Soup
### (for 4–5 portions)

$1/2$ cup mashed potato                    1 tablespoon cornflour

$1^1/_2$ cups milk
1 tablespoon butter
$1^1/_2$ cups Basic Vegetable
  Broth (light)
1 can creamed sweetcorn
$1^1/_2$ teaspoons salt
2 teaspoons vegetable
  bouillon powder

(blended in 3 tablespoons
  water)
$^1/_2$ cup cream
4 egg whites
1 yolk of salted duck egg

Heat the butter and potato in a saucepan. Add the milk slowly. Stir and mix continually until the mixture is well blended. Pour in the broth and creamed sweetcorn. Add the salt, vegetable bouillon powder and cornflour mixture. Stir until the mixture is well mixed. Add the cream, and beat the egg white with a rotary beater until nearly stiff. Stir the egg white into the soup. Heat gently for 2 minutes. Pour the soup into a serving bowl. Garnish with chopped egg yolk and serve.

# Rice

Rice, as a vegetable or vegetarian dish, is prepared and served in four main ways in China: as Vegetable Rice (when the vegetables are cooked or steamed in the rice), as Topped Rice (when a savoury vegetable or vegetarian dish is used as a substantial garnish on top of cooked rice), as Fried Rice (when a number of chopped vegetable items are stir-fried together with cooked rice), and as Soft Rice (also known as Congee, which is a watery rice porridge, with a selection of vegetables slow-simmered in it).

Patna rice is the best type to use for all the recipes that follow, but any long-grained rice will do.

## BASIC BOILED RICE

There are numerous ways in which boiled rice can be successfully cooked. In China it is very often steamed, but in the West two of the easiest ways to prepare it are probably:

(1) Place the rice in a heavy pan. Add water to twice the depth of the rice. Bring to the boil. Simmer very gently for 8 minutes. Turn off the heat, but leave the rice to cook in its own heat for the next 10 minutes, after which it should be ready. Open the lid *only* when the cooking is done or when you are ready to serve.

(2) Alternatively, the rice can be cooked in a casserole. Place the rice in the casserole. Add water to twice the depth of the rice. Bring to the boil, cover the casserole and place in a preheated oven at 180°C (350°F) mark 4 for 10 minutes. Turn off

the heat and leave the rice to cook in its own heat in the casserole, in the oven, for the next 10 minutes.

## VEGETABLE RICE

The so-called Vegetable Rice is cooked in China by adding a given vegetable or vegetables to the rice at the start of the cooking in the proportion of one part vegetable to two parts rice, together with a small amount of salt and oil or butter. The aim of the dish is to produce rice which has been impregnated with the flavour of vegetable. This is not a complete dish in itself; it is usually eaten with 2–3 other savoury vegetable dishes.

### *Spring Green Vegetable Rice*

$3^1/_2$ cups water
1 teaspoon salt
$1^1/_2$–2 tablespoons butter
2 cups rice
$^1/_2$-$^3/_4$ lb spring greens

Clean the greens thoroughly, discard any coarse leaves and root, and cut into 2-inch pieces. Place all the ingredients in a casserole. Bring to the boil, stir contents once and place the casserole in a preheated oven at 180°C (350°F) mark 4 for 15 minutes. Turn off the heat and leave the rice and greens to cook in their own heat for the next 15 minutes.

### *Green Peas and Mushroom Vegetable Rice*

Repeat the previous recipe, using $^1/_2$ lb of green peas and $^1/_4$ lb of mushrooms instead of spring greens. Clean and rinse the mushrooms twice before adding to the rice.

## Carrots, Watercress and Cucumber Vegetable Rice

Repeat recipe (1) using $1/2$ lb each of carrots and cucumber (retain skin). Scrape and dice the carrots and cucumber into $1/4$-inch cubes, and slice $1/4$ lb of watercress at 1-inch intervals. Spread the vegetables under the rice before adding water, at the start of the cooking.

## Bamboo-shoots Vegetable Rice with 'Golden Needles' and Peas

Use $1/2$ lb of fresh or canned bamboo-shoots with $1/4$ lb of dried bamboo-shoots, $1/4$ lb of green peas, and 2 stalks of 'golden needles'. The 'golden needles' must be soaked for 1 hour, drained and cut into 2-inch segments, and the dried bamboo-shoots soaked for the same length of time and cut into $1^1/2$-inch pieces. Otherwise proceed in the same manner as in the previous recipes. (It is customary for the diners to sprinkle Vegetable Rice with a few drops of good quality soya sauce.)

## TOPPED RICE

Topped Rice simply means placing a portion of any one of the stir-fried, red-cooked, white-cooked or marinaded dishes on top of a portion of boiled rice. In fact, almost any savoury dish which has a tasty gravy will be suitable. The dish will be further improved if the dish used for the garnish is supplemented by a few tablespoons of any one of the Vegetable Sauces (see pages 79–84), such as Hot Black Beans and Tomato Sauce, Sweet and Sour Sauce, Mushroom Sauce, Fu-Yung Sauce, Hot Peanut Butter Sauce or even the Willow Sauce (the last is very vinegary). The suitability of Topped Rice for the average Western meal lies in the fact that it is served in individual portions, rather than in the usual Chinese buffet style, where a whole range of dishes – or at least 3–4 – have to be prepared to make up a proper meal.

## FRIED RICE

In non-vegetarian cooking, Fried Rice is made by stir-frying cooked rice with a quantity of chopped onion, chopped ham or bacon and scrambled eggs, the latter items being stir-fried in oil for a while beforehand. In vegetarian cooking, the ham or bacon should be replaced by one or two salted or dried vegetables, such as braised bamboo-shoots, salted turnip or Red-in-Snow, and colour contrast and difference in texture can be introduced by the addition of green peas, chopped mushrooms and sweetcorn. What must always be avoided is a Fried Rice that is so mixed-up that it borders on a mess. To prevent this, many of the items, such as peas, mushrooms and sweetcorn, should be stir-fried separately, including the egg, which should be set first, before they are assembled together in the final stir-frying.

### *Vegetarian Fried Rice*
(for 6 portions)

1 lb cooked rice (must be dry and in separate grains)
4 eggs
$^1/_2$ teaspoon salt
1 large onion
4 oz braised bamboo-shoots
2–3 oz salted or braised turnips (optional)
$1^1/_2$ oz Red-in-Snow pickled greens (optional)

$3^1/_2$ tablespoons vegetable oil
4 oz mushrooms (or 2 oz dried mushrooms)
4 oz green peas
4 oz sweetcorn
2 tablespoons butter
$1^1/_2$ tablespoons soya sauce
$^1/_2$ tablespoon sesame oil

Add the salt to the eggs and beat with a fork for 10 seconds. Dice the bamboo-shoots, turnips, Red-in-Snow and onion into pea-sized cubes. Dice the mushrooms into similar size pieces which should be rinsed in water if fresh, soaked in water first for $^1/_2$ an hour if dried; discard stems.

Heat the onion in $2^1/_2$ tablespoons of oil in a small frying-pan on a medium heat. Stir-fry for 1 minute. Add the beaten egg. Scramble lightly when the egg is about to set. Heat the bamboo-shoots, turnips and Red-in-Snow in a tablespoon of oil in another pan for 1 minute. Add the butter, mushrooms, sweetcorn and peas. Stir-fry together for 2 minutes.

Heat the rice in a large saucepan on a medium heat for 1 minute. Add the lightly scrambled egg. Toss and turn to mix it with the rice. Pour all the other ingredients into the rice. Pour in good quality soya sauce and sesame oil. Stir, turn and mix them all together, still on a medium heat. Lift the rice slightly each time you stir and turn, so that it will not stick. Toss and stir for 2 minutes. The aim in Fried Rice is to produce a colourful dish of rice which is light, tasty and aromatic. In fact, Fried Rice might be described as a hot 'rice salad'.

## Fried Rice (B)
### (for 6 portions)

1 lb cooked rice (boiled)
1 large onion
3 oz braised bamboo-shoots
2 oz bamboo-shoots (canned or fresh)
4 fresh eggs
$^1/_2$ teaspoon salt
4 tablespoons vegetable oil
2 oz raisins
4 oz mushrooms (or 2 oz dried mushrooms)
1 tablespoon butter
4 oz green peas
4 oz sweetcorn
2 salted duck eggs
2 stalks spring onion
$1^1/_2$ tablespoons soya sauce

Cut the onion into thin slices and the spring onion into $^1/_2$-inch segments using all the green parts. Dice the bamboo-shoots, braised bamboo-shoots and mushrooms into pea-sized cubes. Chop the salted eggs into similar size cubes. Add the salt to the fresh eggs and beat for 10 seconds with a fork.

Stir-fry the onion in $2^1/_2$ tablespoons of oil in a frying-pan for 1 minute on a medium heat; pour in the beaten eggs. Scramble the egg lightly just before it has set. Remove from heat and keep hot.

Heat 2 tablespoons of oil in another frying-pan. Add the bamboo-shoots and mushrooms and stir-fry together for $1^1/_2$ minutes. Add the butter, peas, sweetcorn and raisins. Stir-fry them together for 2 minutes. Heat the rice in a large saucepan on a medium heat. Pour in the contents of both frying-pans. Turn and stir until all the items are well mixed. Lift the mixture each time you turn it and stir the rice to ensure that it is light and separated. Sprinkle the chopped salted egg, spring onion and soya sauce over the rice. Turn a few times more and serve.

## CONGEE (OR SOFT RICE)

Plain Soft Rice or Congee, like porridge, is usually eaten at breakfast time in China, accompanied by such things as roasted peanuts (salted), pickled vegetables, soya-marinaded vegetables, salted preserved eggs, etc. Savoury Soft Rice is usually eaten as a snack. There is a great variety of Savoury Soft Rice, especially for non-vegetarians, since there are a great variety of savoury foods which can be cooked and simmered in Soft Rice to make it very tasty and appetizing. For vegetarians the variations are more limited, being confined to the number of vegetables that can be cooked with Soft Rice to make the latter truly interesting: these are a combination of nuts with root and leaf vegetables, together with the salted, pickled and soya-braised vegetables.

## Basic Soft Rice

$^1/_2$ lb rice
4–5 pints water
  (quantity depending
  upon the thickness

of the the Soft Rice which is
required)

Wash and rinse the rice a couple of times. Place it in a heavy pan and add water. Bring to the boil and reduce heat to a minimum. Leave the rice to simmer very gently for $1^1/_2$–2 hours, stirring with a wooden spoon every 15–20 minutes. By the end of this time the Soft Rice will have become a thickish gruel, which is extremely bland on the tongue. It is this blandness which gives it a refreshing quality, making it ideal for eating with great relish with salty, preserved and highly savoury foods.

## Savoury Soft Rice (A)

$^1/_2$ lb rice
4–5 pints water
$^1/_4$ lb peanuts
$^1/_4$ lb carrots
$^1/_2$ lb cabbage
1 teaspoon salt
3 tablespoons Red-in-Snow
  pickled greens

2 salted duck eggs
2 tablespoons soya sauce
1 teaspoon bean-curd (tofu)
  cheese
$^1/_2$ teaspoon vegetable
  bouillon powder
2 teaspoons sesame oil

Prepare the Basic Soft Rice in the same manner as in the previous recipe. Clean the carrots and cabbage thoroughly. Dice the carrots and eggs into $^1/_4$-inch cubes and cut the cabbage, including most of the stem, into 2-inch pieces. After the rice has been cooking for $^1/_2$ an hour, add the peanuts, salt and carrots. Add cabbage $^1/_2$ an hour later. When the Soft Rice is almost ready, stir in the pickled greens, duck eggs, soya sauce, tofu cheese, vegetable bouillon powder and sesame oil. Savoury Soft Rice made in this way can be eaten on its own, but more often it is eaten with two or three savoury dishes, vegetarian or non-vegetarian.

### Savoury Soft Rice (B)
(for 4–6 portions)

$^1/_2$ lb rice
4–5 pints water
4–6 eggs
6 oz water chestnuts
6 oz watercress
4–6 tablespoons soya sauce
12 tablespoons Hot Black
  Beans and Tomato Sauce
  (see page 79)

2 tablespoons butter
2 tablespoons light soya
  sauce
$^1/_2$ teaspoon vegetable
  bouillon powder

Prepare the Basic Soft Rice as in the previous recipes. Cut the water chestnuts into thin slices. Clean and slice the watercress at $1^1/_2$-inch intervals.

After the rice has cooked for $^1/_2$ an hour, add the water chestnuts. Half an hour later, add the watercress, butter, soya sauce and vegetable bouillon powder. Just before the Soft Rice is ready to serve, break the eggs into it to poach.

Divide the Soft Rice into 4–6 bowls, each with a poached egg. Pour over each egg 1 tablespoon of soya sauce and 2 tablespoons of Hot Black Beans and Tomato Sauce, and serve.

### Savoury Soft Rice (C)
(for 4–6 portions)

$^1/_2$–$^3/_4$ lb rice
4–5 pints water
4 salted duck eggs
10 oz bean sprouts

4 tablespoons soya sauce
2 tablespoons butter
9 tablespoons Mushroom
  Sauce (see page 82)

| | |
|---|---|
| 6 large Chinese dried mushrooms | 2 tablespoons light soya sauce |
| 4 tablespoons Red-in-Snow pickled greens | $1/2$ teaspoon vegetable bouillon powder (optional) |

Clean the bean sprouts thoroughly and drain. Chop the Red-in-Snow into coarse grains. Soak the dried mushrooms for $1/2$ an hour, slice into matchstick strips and discard stems. Cut each salted egg into 10 slices and then quarter each slice.

Prepare the Basic Soft Rice as in the previous recipes. When it has cooked for $1^1/2$ hours, add the salted egg, bean sprouts, mushroom strips, soya sauce and vegetable bouillon powder. Add the Red-in-Snow and butter 5 minutes before serving. Stir gently until all the ingredients are well mixed.

Divide the Soft Rice into 4–6 bowls. Pour just under 1 tablespoon of soya sauce and 2 tablespoons of Mushroom Sauce into each bowl and serve. Keep any balance hot for second helpings.

# Pastas

Pastas rank next to rice as the most important staple food of China. They come mostly in three forms: (a) noodles (*Mein*); (b) wraplings (*Chiaotze*) and (c) steamed buns (*Paotze*).

## NOODLES

Noodles may be served in soups, in sauce, or fried (Chow Mein); or they can be hot tossed.

### Tossed Noodles (A)
(for 3–4 portions)

| | |
|---|---|
| 1 lb noodles (or spaghetti) | 6 tablespoons Mushroom |
| 2 stalks spring onion | Sauce (see page 82) |
| 2 tablespoons butter | 6 oz bean sprouts |
| 3 tablespoons soya sauce | 6 oz cucumber |
| $1/_2$ tablespoon soya paste | 4 oz radish |
| $1/_2$ tablespoon hoisin sauce | $1/_2$ small bowl vinegar (with |
| $1^1/_2$ teaspoons sugar | 1 tablespoon sesame oil |
| 2 tablespoons sherry | added) |
| 3 tablespoons vegetable oil | 1 tablespoon Vegetable Broth |

Cut the spring onions into $1/_2$-inch segments. Rinse and clean the bean sprouts. Boil the noodles (20 minutes for spaghetti, 7–8 minutes for noodles), drain and keep hot. Add the butter, sprinkle with spring onion, toss and divide into 3–4 bowls – one bowl for each person. Heat the oil in a small frying-pan on a medium heat. Add the soya sauce, soya paste, hoisin sauce, sugar, Vegetable Broth and sherry. Stir for 50 seconds or until the mixture is consistent.

Shred the cucumber and radish into matchstick-sized strips. Place them and the bean sprouts in separate bowls.

Place one bowl of noodles in front of each person. Pour into each bowl $1^1/_2$ tablespoons of Mushroom Sauce (hot) and $1^1/_2$ tablespoons of the mixed sauce from the pan. Pour the remainder of the mixed sauce into a bowl. Place the various bowls of bean sprouts, cucumber, radish and vinegar alongside the bowl of mixed sauce for the diners to help themselves. After taking a helping from each bowl, the diner tosses the raw vegetable strips and sesame oil and vinegar with the sauces and cooked noodles already in his bowl. The interest in such a dish lies in the contrast between the raw crunchy vegetable strips and the softness of the noodles, and also between the blandness of the noodles and the sharpness of the sauces and aromatic vinegar. Naturally the quantity of sauces and ingredients can be varied according to taste.

## Tossed Noodles (B)

Repeat the previous recipe, using 6–7 tablespoons of Hot Black Beans and Tomato Sauce (see page 79) and 4 tablespoons of Hot Peanut Butter Sauce (see page 84) instead of the Mushroom Sauce and the made-up sauce. When the noodles are first tossed with the chopped spring onion and butter, an additional tablespoon of hot salad oil should be added. Otherwise the noodles should be served in the same manner as in the previous recipe, leaving the diner to make his own choice of the quantities of raw vegetable strips and vinegar and sesame oil to be tossed with his or her own bowl of noodles.

# CHOW MEIN (OR FRIED NOODLES)

The difference between Tossed Noodles and Fried Noodles
(Chow Mein) lies in the fact that in the case of the latter,
the different ingredients are not mixed with the noodles by the
diner, but by the cook in the kitchen. With Fried Noodles
the mixing is done in a hot frying-pan with more oil, with
one or more crunchy ingredients such as strips of shredded
bamboo-shoots, cabbage, bean sprouts, onions, etc., added.
Just before serving a quantity of savoury ingredients (with
vegetarians usually stir-fried or braised foods) are placed on
top of the noodles – mushrooms, French beans, celery, cabbage, peas, pea pods, spinach, pickles, etc. These savoury
ingredients should consist of about $^1/_4$–$^1/_3$ of the weight of the
noodles themselves. Thus Chow Mein or Fried Noodles is in
fact a kind of 'double-decker' dish.

## Chow Mein (A)
### (for 3–4 portions)

| | |
|---|---|
| 1 lb noodles (or spaghetti) | 4 large Chinese dried |
| 3 tablespoons vegetable oil | mushrooms |
| 1 tablespoon butter | 3 oz bamboo-shoots |
| 1–2 cloves garlic | 3–4 oz cabbage |
| 1 medium-size onion | 4 oz mushrooms |
| 2 tablespoons soya sauce | $^1/_2$ teaspoon sugar |
| 4 tablespoons Hot Black | 1 tablespoon soya sauce |
| Beans and Tomato Sauce | $^1/_4$ tablespoon hoisin sauce |
| (see page 79) | 1 tablespoon sherry |
| $^1/_2$ tablespoon sesame oil | pepper (to taste) |
| 2 tablespoons butter | |

Boil the noodles (for 7–8 minutes) or spaghetti (for 12–15
minutes), drain and rinse under running water to prevent
sticking. Crush garlic, and slice the onion into thin slices. Slice

the bamboo-shoots and cabbage into $1/4$-inch-long strips and parboil for 3 minutes. Soak the dried mushrooms for $1/2$ an hour, remove the stalks and slice into matchstick strips. Wash and slice the mushrooms into similar strips, discarding the stalks.

Heat the oil and 1 tablespoon of butter in a frying-pan on a medium heat. Add the garlic and onion and stir-fry for 1 minute. Add the cabbage and bamboo-shoots and continue to stir-fry for 3 minutes. Add the cooked noodles, sprinkle with the soya sauce, turn and mix with the oil, bamboo-shoots and cabbage on a medium heat for 3–4 minutes, until the ingredients are cooked through and well mixed. Spread the fried noodles, etc., on a well-heated serving dish and keep hot in the oven. Heat the Hot Black Beans and Tomato Sauce in a small pan on a low heat with sesame oil.

Heat the butter in a small pan on a medium heat. Add the dried mushrooms and stir-fry for 1 minute. Add the mushrooms and stir-fry for another minute. Add 1 tablespoon of soya sauce, hoisin sauce, sherry, pepper and sugar. Stir-fry them together for 2 minutes.

Pour the mushrooms over the centre of the hot noodles. Pour the Hot Black Beans and Tomato Sauce in a circle around the mushrooms. Place in the centre of the table for the diners to help themselves.

## Chow Mein (B)
### (for 3–4 portions)

Repeat the previous recipe, using 3 oz of braised bamboo-shoots (available in cans) and 6 oz of bean sprouts instead of bamboo-shoots and cabbage for a crunchy effect. Mushroom Sauce (see page 82) can be used instead of Black Beans and Tomato Sauce.

Alternatively 2–3 oz of Mange-tout (pea pods) or French beans, cut into 1–2-inch segments, and 2 oz of green peas can be added to be stir-fried with the mushrooms for an additional couple of minutes, with a slight increase of flavouring ingredients, and used as garnish along with the mushrooms. The use of fresh peas and beans should help to increase the colour appeal of the dish. While stir-frying, a couple of tablespoons of Vegetable Broth, $^1/_4$ teaspoon of vegetable bouillon powder and $^1/_2$ teaspoon of chilli sauce may be added.

For non-vegetarians, the noodles are usually stir-fried with 3–4 oz of meat – pork or chicken cut into matchstick strips, stir-fried with garlic and onion at the outset; and items such as shredded beef, lamb, crab meat and prawns can be added to stir-fry with mushrooms, beans and peas, and used as a garnish.

Such a 'double-decker' combination usually provides a reasonably substantial snack in China. The excellence of such a dish, vegetarian or otherwise, depends on the freshness and savouriness of the garnish used, and the right combination of the crunchiness and taste of the vegetables mixed with the softness of the noodles. When these combinations are right the dish becomes a classic. But they can also develop into a mess, if the separate cooking procedure is not followed and everything is put in to stir-fry together.


## WRAPLINGS (OR CHIAOTZE)

Wraplings are foods or stuffings wrapped in thin dough-skin, in the form of a pouch about the size but half the thickness of an average egg. Wraplings (or *Chiaotze*) are usually steamed or boiled, and occasionally fried, or sometimes part-steamed and part-fried. They are eaten as snacks. In North China, when a dozen or a score of them are consumed at a time, they are treated as a meal. The dough-skin of wraplings should be thin and lightly brushed with oil. When made in this way they become somewhat transparent when cooked. Almost any kind of savoury food can be used as stuffing, but those which require longer cooking should be stir-fried first before they are wrapped in the dough-skin.

## Wrapling Skin

| | |
|---|---|
| 1 lb plain flour | 2 cups boiling water |
| 1 teaspoon salt | $^1/_2$ cup vegetable oil |

Sift the flour and salt into a basin. Stir in the boiling water slowly and blend until the mixture is smooth. Cover the basin with a lid and leave to stand for $^1/_2$ an hour.

Place the dough on a well-oiled board, and knead with hands and fingers which have been rubbed with oil. Knead until the dough has become bouncy and elastic. Roll the dough into a roll of about 1 inch in diameter, cut off $^1/_4$-inch discs and form each into a small ball. Flatten these with a rolling-pin into a pancake about 3–3$^1/_2$ inches in diameter. Place the stuffing (1–2 teaspoonfuls) just below the centre of the pancake. Fold over from the bottom up, and pinch the edges together by puckering them and pressing them together. Beaten egg can be used to help the sealing if necessary.

## Stuffing

In non-vegetarian cooking, all kinds of meats, fish and sea-foods are commonly used as stuffings. In vegetarian cooking, the most frequently used stuffings are mushrooms, dried mushrooms (soaked), celery, Chinese cabbage, tofu, spinach, watercress, young leeks, spring onion, braised bamboo-shoots, braised tofu and Red-in-Snow pickled greens. These items of stuffing will naturally require some seasoning with salt, pepper, soya sauce, sugar, wine, sesame oil and vegetable bouillon powder after they have been shredded into broad strips. Mushrooms and dried mushrooms must be shredded and stir-fried in butter for a couple of minutes. Red-in-Snow is usually chopped coarsely and sprinkled in small quantities over the other ingredients, to provide greater piquancy.

When a sufficient number of these wraplings have been made (calculate six to each person for a snack and a dozen each for a meal), brush them lightly with salad oil, place them on a well-greased surface in a steamer and steam for 15 minutes; they may also be boiled in a large pan of boiling water for 10–12 minutes, adding 4 or 5 at a time.

Wraplings can be served in soups (like stuffed dumplings), or they can be served as they are, usually with bowls or dishes of soya sauce mixed with vinegar placed on the table for the diners to dip the wraplings in.

The wraplings can be placed in a well-greased frying-pan or griddle and heated on a medium heat for 4–5 minutes until the bottoms are slightly browned. Wraplings cooked in this way are favourites in Peking, where they are called *Kuo Tieh*. In China all the family joins in making these wraplings.

A typical bowl of stuffing for 2 dozen wraplings can be made as follows:

1 bean-curd (tofu) cake
6 medium-size Chinese dried
  mushrooms
3 oz mushrooms
2 stalks spring onion
4 oz leaf spinach
4 oz Chinese cabbage (or
  young Savoy)
1 oz Red-in-Snow pickled
  greens

$^1/_2$ teaspoon vegetable
  bouillon powder
$1^1/_2$ tablespoons soya sauce
1 teaspoon sugar
$1^1/_2$ tablespoons butter
$^1/_2$ teaspoon salt
$1^1/_2$ tablespoons sesame oil
pepper (to taste)

Soak the dried mushrooms for $^1/_2$ an hour, discard stalks and shred into matchstick-size strips. Chop the fresh mushrooms to the same size. Cut the tofu into similar pieces. Cut the spring onion into 1-inch segments.

Cut the cabbage and spinach into $^1/_2$-inch slices. Place them in a large basin. Chop the Red-in-Snow coarsely. Sprinkle the vegetables with salt, vegetable bouillon powder, Red-in-Snow and sesame oil. Knead with the fingers and leave to season for $^1/_2$ an hour.

Heat the butter in a frying-pan. Add the spring onion and dried mushroom. Stir-fry them together on a medium heat for $1^1/_2$ minutes. Add the tofu and mushrooms, and sprinkle with soya sauce and sugar. Stir-fry them all together for 2 minutes. Add the contents of the frying-pan into the basin and mix the 2 groups of ingredients together. Use as stuffing for wraplings.


## STEAMED BUNS (OR PAOTZE)

These 'steamed buns' are much bigger affairs than wraplings; they are about the size of an average orange, but a little squatter in shape like mandarins or tangerines. To Westerners, who are used to baked buns and breads, these are a little unusual, because since they are steamed they are white or cream in colour and soft to the touch. When well made they are very palatable and since they can be eaten cold, they can serve as sandwiches and be eaten at picnics. As with wraplings, almost anything under the sun can be used as stuffing, so long as it is edible, palatable and delicious. Non-vegetarians commonly use cooked meats, vegetables and seafoods. Vegetarians use the same type of stuffing used in wraplings (see previous recipe), except that larger quantities are required: about 3–4 teaspoonfuls.

## Steamed Buns (A)

### FOR DOUGH-SKIN

1 lb flour

$^1/_2$ teaspoon salt

$1^1/_2$ teaspoons baking
  powder

2 teaspoons sugar

$2^1/_2$ cups water (warm)

### FOR STUFFING

As in the previous recipe

Sift the flour, salt, baking powder and sugar into a large basin. Stir in the water, and mix with a wooden spoon. Form the dough into a ball and allow to stand for $^1/_2$ an hour. Knead the dough on a well-greased surface, working it thoroughly until it is elastic and bouncy. Cover with a damp cloth and leave to develop for a further 1 hour.

Form the dough into a 2-inch-diameter roll. Slice off $^1/_2$-inch discs and press to increase the diameter to approximately $3^1/_2$ inches. Make a slight indentation in the centre of the disc with the back of a spoon. Place 3–4 teaspoons of stuffing in the indentation. Gradually and gently gather the sides of the dough-disc upwards until they have covered the stuffing completely (as the sides are brought together they should become somewhat creased or puckered). Place each bun on a small piece of greased paper.

Place the buns in a single layer, each sitting on a piece of greased paper, in a steamer, and steam steadily for 30 minutes. They can either be eaten immediately or be served cold.

## Steamed Buns (B)

Use a different stuffing by substituting bean sprouts and watercress for spinach, and celery for cabbage. In the stir-frying of the mushrooms and tofu a couple of tablespoons of Hot Black Beans and Tomato Sauce (see page 79) may be added.

For non-vegetarians, 4–5 oz of shredded chicken meat, pork, lamb or crab meat can be added to stir-fry with the mushrooms – omitting the tofu – for an extra minute or two, then combined and mixed with the vegetables for use as stuffing. The result is highly appetizing.

# Eggs

In every cuisine in the world eggs occupy an important place. Served in their original shape, eggs usually come in three forms in China: salted egg (usually duck egg), soya egg (browned egg) and preserved egg (the '1000-year-old' variety). All these can be prepared at home, but these days the average Chinese housewife would no more think of making salted and preserved eggs at home than would the average Western housewife think of making butter or margarine in her own kitchen. Soya eggs, however, are almost always made at home, probably because they are so easy to do. The three types of egg are always appetizing when served together in the same dish, if only because of their quite different tastes and difference in colour: the salted egg is white and yellow, the soya egg is brown, and the preserved egg is a yellow-green-and-golden-translucent brown. They are most often served for breakfast or midnight supper. Because of their strong flavour they are excellent with the blandness of plain rice (usually with Congee or Soft Rice, or rice gruel). Otherwise the majority of egg dishes are produced by stir-frying or steaming.

### Soya Eggs

6 eggs                                    1 pint soya sauce

Hard boil the eggs and shell them. Heat the soya sauce in a saucepan. When it is just about to boil, lower the eggs into the sauce. Leave to simmer for 15 minutes. Turn off the heat and leave the eggs to cool in the sauce for $^1/_2$ an hour.

Drain away the soya sauce and reserve for other uses. Slice each egg carefully into quarters or sixths, arrange yolk side up on a serving dish and serve.

## Steamed Four Types of Egg
### (for 6–8 portions)

2 soya eggs
2 salted eggs
2 preserved eggs
2 fresh eggs
$^3/_4$ pint Clear-simmer Broth
 (cold; see page 73)

$^1/_4$ teaspoon vegetable
 bouillon powder
$^1/_2$ teaspoon salt
pepper (to taste)
1 stalk spring onion
$1^1/_2$ teaspoons sesame oil

Beat the fresh eggs with a fork for 10 seconds. Add the broth, salt, pepper and vegetable bouillon powder and beat again until well blended. Shell the salted and preserved eggs. Cut each egg into quarters, including the soya eggs. Chop the spring onion coarsely.

Arrange the three types of egg, yolk side up, in one layer on a flat, heatproof dish. Pour the beaten egg mixture over them until they are nearly all covered. Place the dish in a steamer and steam for 15 minutes, by which time the surface of the beaten egg mixture will have jelled. Sprinkle the eggs with the chopped spring onion and sesame oil. Steam for another 2–3 minutes and serve in the dish.

## Plain Steamed Egg
### (for 3–4 portions)

2 eggs
1 pint Clear-simmer Broth
 (see page 73)
1 teaspoon salt
pepper (to taste)

$^1/_2$ teaspoon sugar
1 teaspoon vegetable oil
1 tablespoon sherry
1 tablespoon soya sauce

$^1/_2$ teaspoon vegetable  bouillon powder

$^1/_2$ tablespoon chopped  chives

Beat the eggs, broth, salt, pepper, sugar, vegetable bouillon powder and oil together with a fork for 20–30 seconds until thoroughly blended. Place the mixture in a 2–3-inch deep heatproof dish. Place the dish in a steamer, and steam for 20 minutes.

Sprinkle the top of the steamed egg with sherry, soya sauce and chopped chives, and steam for an extra minute. Serve in the original dish.

## Steamed Eggs with Vegetables

The majority of vegetables, which require comparatively short cooking, can be steamed with and in the egg and broth mixture: vegetables such as spinach, mushrooms, celery and bean sprouts. It is usually best to rub the vegetables with a little salt and oil first and leave them to season for 10 minutes before placing them at the bottom of the heatproof dish and pouring on the beaten egg/broth mixture. The vegetables, singly or in combination, should not exceed in volume half the quantity of the egg/broth mixture; otherwise they tend to exude too much water when cooked, and after all the dish is meant to be an egg one. Another favourite for sprinkling over the egg a couple of minutes before serving is Red-in-Snow pickled greens (a tablespoon or two chopped coarsely).

For non-vegetarians, there are a great variety of cooked foods which can be combined with steamed eggs. These include practically all the meats, particularly chopped smoked ham, bacon, roast pork, Chinese sausage, minced beef and chicken, as well as most fish and seafoods, flaked fish – cod, smoked haddock, etc. – crab, lobster, oyster, shrimps, etc. The combination can be done in two ways: either by mixing these ingredients with the beaten egg/broth, or alternatively, by stir-frying them for a short period in a small quantity of oil and using them as garnish. They are steamed for a minute or two on the dish before it is served. Some of the ingredients can be steamed in the egg/broth mixture, and the rest stir-fried and used as garnish.

### Basic Stir-fried Egg
(for 5–6 portions)

| | |
|---|---|
| 5 or 6 eggs | 3 tablespoons vegetable oil |
| 1 teaspoon salt | 1 tablespoon butter |
| 2 stalks spring onion | $1^1/_2$ tablespoons sherry |
| pepper (to taste) | |

Chop the onion into $^1/_4$-inch pieces. Add these along with the salt and pepper to the eggs. Beat for 10 seconds.

Heat the oil and butter in a frying-pan. When hot, lower to medium heat and add the egg mixture. As the egg begins to set, lift the edges up with a spoon or spatula and draw towards the centre, so that the still liquid egg on top will flow outwards and underneath. Just as the remainder of the egg is about to set, pour in the sherry from the side. Turn immediately on to a well-heated dish and serve at once. The addition of a small quantity of sherry at the last moment gives rise to a most appetizing 'bouquet', which combines with the aroma of the freshly chopped spring onion to give this simple dish its distinction.

## STIR-FRIED EGGS WITH VEGETABLES

Stir-fried eggs can be combined successfully with a good range of vegetables, such as spinach, tomatoes, mushrooms, bean sprouts, peas and French beans. The best way to prepare them is probably to stir-fry the eggs and vegetables in separate frying-pans, and to combine them in one pan at the moment they are ready, adding the contents of the egg pan to the pan containing the vegetables. The stir-fried eggs should be prepared as in the previous recipe, and the vegetables should be stir-fried, seasoned with soya sauce and hoisin sauce (1 tablespoon of soya sauce and $^1/_2$ tablespoon of hoisin sauce and $^1/_2$ teaspoon of sugar to $^3/_4$ lb of vegetables, plus 2 tablespoons of oil and 1 of butter). When stir-fried for $2^1/_2$–3 minutes on a high heat the vegetables should be sufficiently cooked, with some gravy left in the pan. When the contents of the egg pan are added to the vegetables and turned and tossed lightly together, the dish should present an attractive contrast between the bright yellow of egg and the green, red, brown or whatever the colour of vegetables they are cooked with. The contrast between the flavour and texture of the eggs and the vegetables also helps to enhance the dish. A teaspoon or two of sesame oil, and an extra tablespoonful of sherry and soya sauce may be added to the sizzling pan just before the dish is served. These add to the distinct aromatic appeal.

### Stir-fried Eggs with Spinach
(for 4–6 portions)

| | |
|---|---|
| 4 eggs | 3 tablespoons vegetable oil |
| $^1/_2$ teaspoon salt | $1^1/_2$ tablespoons soya sauce |
| 2 stalks spring onion | $^1/_2$ tablespoon hoisin sauce |
| pepper (to taste) | $^1/_2$ teaspoon sugar |
| $2^1/_2$ tablespoons butter | 2 tablespoons sherry |
| $^3/_4$ lb spinach | 2 teaspoons sesame oil |

Use 2 frying-pans (or 1 frying-pan and 1 saucepan for spinach). Prepare and cook the eggs in the same manner as in the previous recipe, without adding the sherry.

Prepare the spinach by washing and draining thoroughly

and removing the stems, using only the leaves. Remove any discoloured leaves.

Heat the oil in a frying-pan or saucepan on a high heat. When the oil is very hot, add the spinach, and turn it briskly in the oil for $2^1/_2$ minutes. Add the soya sauce, hoisin sauce and sugar, and continue to stir-fry for 1 minute.

Add the contents of the egg pan to the spinach. Stir and turn, keeping the heat at high. Add the sherry and sesame oil. Turn once more and serve.

All the other dishes of stir-fried eggs with vegetables can be prepared and cooked in more or less the same manner, stir-frying the eggs and vegetables separately and combining them at the last moment, with the blessing of sherry and sesame oil just before serving.

Sweet and Sour Sauce (see page 81) is often added to stir-fried eggs or plain-fried eggs. It can simply be poured on the egg dishes just before serving. The egginess of eggs and the Sweet and Sour Sauce seem to combine well. Hot Black Beans and Tomato Sauce (page 79) is another sauce which can be used with most stir-fried egg dishes.

## EGG FU-YUNG

In the West, 'Egg Fu-Yung' seems to apply to all manner of Chinese egg dishes. But in China it is really only applicable to dishes which are produced with beaten egg white cooked with other ingredients (for non-vegetarians, often minced chicken or minced flaked fish meat are combined and beaten together with egg white). In Western terms, Egg Fu-Yung should really be called Chinese 'egg-white soufflé'.

## Cauliflower Fu-Yung
(for 4–6 portions)

1 medium-size cauliflower
1 tablespoon light soya sauce
3 tablespoons Clear-simmer
  Broth (see page 73)
2 tablespoons butter
4 egg whites

2 teaspoons cornflour
$1/_2$ teaspoon salt
$1/_2$ teaspoon vegetable
  bouillon powder
3 tablespoons top of milk or
  cream
6 tablespoons vegetable oil

Break the cauliflower into individual florets. Parboil for 3 minutes and drain. Sprinkle evenly with soya sauce. Beat the egg white with a rotary beater together with the salt, vegetable bouillon powder and cornflour until nearly stiff but not dry. Add the cream or top of the milk and continue to mix and beat together for a short while (3–4 seconds).

Heat the butter in a saucepan (or frying-pan). Add the cauliflower, broth and seasoning ingredients. Stir-fry on a high heat for 2 minutes. Heat the oil in a frying-pan. When hot, reduce the heat to medium, add the beaten egg white and turn it in the oil. Turn until the egg is set. Drain away the excess oil and return the pan to the heat. Pour and fold the contents of the cauliflower pan into the egg white. Turn and mix gently for 1 minute. Turn out on to a well-heated dish and serve.

## French Beans Fu-Yung
(for 4–6 portions)

1 lb French beans
1 tablespoon light soya sauce
3 tablespoons Clear-simmer
  Broth (page 73)
pepper (to taste)
2 tablespoons butter
4 egg whites

2 teaspoons cornflour
$1/_2$ teaspoon salt
$1/_2$ teaspoon vegetable
  bouillon powder
3 tablespoons single cream
6 tablespoons vegetable oil

This recipe can be prepared and cooked in the same manner as the previous one by preparing and stir-frying the French beans separately from the Fu-Yung (like the cauliflower in the previous recipe, the French beans will require 3 minutes parboiling before stir-frying) and combining and folding them into the Fu-Yung for a minute or two before serving.

For non-vegetarians, the Fu-Yung can be and is often combined with shrimps, crab meat, flaked fish or minced chicken and pork. Sometimes these other ingredients are heavily overlaid with quantities of Fu-Yung, so that the shrimps and crabs or lobster appear to be buried in a thick layer of savoury white 'snow'!

## FLOWING-RUNNING EGG (LIU HUANG TSAI)

This is a type of egg dish which is designed to be eaten with rice. Because the dish is smooth, runny and tasty, it acts as a highly savoury 'lubricant' for the rice, often the principal part of a Chinese meal.

### Flowing-running Egg
(for 4–6 portions)

5 eggs
$^1/_3$ teaspoon salt
$^1/_2$ teaspoon vegetable
  bouillon powder
3 teaspoons cornflour
$^1/_4$ pint Clear-simmer Broth
  (page 73)
pepper (to taste)
$2^1/_2$ tablespoons butter

$3^1/_2$ tablespoons vegetable oil
$1^1/_2$ tablespoons sherry
1 bean-curd (tofu) cake
2 cloves garlic
4 Chinese dried mushrooms
1 tablespoon light soya sauce
4 tablespoons green peas
$1^1/_2$ tablespoons sesame oil

Soak the mushrooms for $^1/_2$ an hour, remove the stems, and cut each mushroom into 6–8 pieces. Chop and mash the tofu. Crush and chop the garlic. Beat the eggs with a fork for 10 seconds. Add the salt, soya sauce, vegetable bouillon powder, pepper, cornflour and broth. Beat together until well blended and smooth.

Melt the butter and 1 tablespoon of oil in a saucepan. When the butter has melted, pour in the egg mixture. Stir slowly but continuously on a medium heat with a wooden spoon until the mixture is quite thick (5–7 minutes). Heat $2^1/_2$ tablespoons of oil in a small saucepan. Add the garlic and mushrooms and stir-fry for 1 minute. Add the green peas, stir and turn them with the mushrooms for $^1/_2$ a minute. Pour in the mashed tofu and sesame oil. Stir the contents for 2 minutes. Pour the mixed contents into the egg mixture. Stir and mix them all together for 1 minute. Add the sherry, stir once more and serve in a bowl as an accompaniment to steamed or boiled rice.

The only difference between the non-vegetarian and the vegetarian version of Flowing-running Egg is that in the former, chicken broth is used instead of Clear-simmer Broth, and 4–5 oz of minced chicken or pork is added to stir-fry with the mushrooms for an extra couple of minutes, before they are combined with the other ingredients in the dish. Half a tablespoon of light soya sauce can be added when stir-frying the mushrooms, peas, and tofu together. This is a favourite dish in Peking.

### Iron Pot (Grown) Egg
#### (for 4–6 portions)

The dish was given its name because the eggs 'grow' in the iron pot (casserole) during cooking. The dish is in fact a soufflé and can be cooked in a heatproof glass bowl in the oven.

| | |
|---|---|
| 5 eggs | 4 large Chinese dried |
| 1 teaspoon salt | mushrooms |

$^1/_2$ teaspoon vegetable
  bouillon powder
2 tablespoons cornflour
1$^1/_2$ teaspoons baking
  powder
$^1/_3$ pint Clear-simmer Broth
  (page 73)
3 tablespoons green peas

2 medium-size tomatoes
$^1/_2$ tablespoon sesame oil
2 tablespoons grated or
  powdered cheese
$^1/_2$ cup milk
2 tablespoons butter
  (clarified)

Skin and dice each tomato into a dozen equal size cubes. Soak the mushrooms for $^1/_2$ an hour, remove the stalks and cut each mushroom into $^1/_2$ a dozen pieces. Beat the eggs in a basin with a rotary beater for 10 seconds. Add all the ingredients and beat for a further 20 seconds.

Pour the egg mixture into a heatproof, well-greased dish, filling only one-third of the dish and thus leaving room for expansion. Place the dish in a preheated oven at 180°C (350°F) mark 4 for 30–35 minutes. During that time the eggs should have 'grown' or expanded two or threefold, in other words risen like a soufflé. The dish must be served and eaten before it collapses.

## Tea Eggs
### (for 6–8 portions)

6–8 eggs
water for boiling
3 tablespoons India tea

1 tablespoon salt
1$^1/_2$ pints water

Hard boil the eggs gently for 8–9 minutes. Leave to cool in the boiling water. When cool, tap gently with a spoon to crack, but not break, the entire shell of the eggs.

Heat 1$^1/_2$ pints of water in a saucepan. When it boils, add tea and salt. Stir and immerse the eggs in the salted tea. Leave to simmer very gently for $^1/_4$ of an hour. Turn the heat off and leave the eggs to stand in the tea for 2 hours.

Pour away the tea, drain the eggs, and shell when cool. Slice each egg lengthwise into quarters and serve for breakfast, late supper, or just as a snack. Tea eggs are also known as 'Marble eggs' because the tea which seeps through the cracked shell during boiling leaves a pattern on the egg just like the patterns one sees on marble.

# Bean-curd (Tofu)

Bean-curd, often called tofu, is one of the basic foods of the Chinese, as it is of the Japanese. It is a creamy coloured, custard-like, slightly spongy substance, generally sold in shops (available from most of the Chinese food stores and supermarkets in the UK and USA) in cakes of about $2^1/_2$–3 inches square and an inch thick. It is in itself fairly bland in taste – and therefore not necessarily immediately appealing to the average Western palate – but it is a great absorber of other tastes and flavours and can be cooked with almost every known food, whether fish, flesh, fowl or vegetables. When so cooked, it becomes, to the Chinese and Japanese at least, a great accompaniment to rice. For connoisseurs even the very blandness of the bean-curd itself tastes attractive. Its high protein value is well known.

Tofu cheese is salted fomented tofu with a strong cheesy flavour. The colour is unimportant.

### Cold Bean-Curd
(for 4–6 portions)

| | |
|---|---|
| 4 cakes bean-curd | $2^1/_2$ tablespoons soya sauce |
| 2 pints water | 2 tablespoons peanut oil |

Cut each bean-curd into four pieces. Place them in a wire basket. Immerse in boiling water to simmer for 3 minutes and drain. Place the pieces of bean-curd on a serving dish. Blend the soya sauce with the peanut oil and pour the mixture over the bean-curd. For variation, a small amount of chilli oil (or

1–1$^1/_2$ teaspoons of chilli sauce) may be blended with the soya sauce and peanut oil mixture.

For non-vegetarians, add 1 tablespoon of shrimp sauce or oyster sauce to the sauce mixture.

### Cold Bean-Curd with Sesame Paste (or Peanut Butter)

Repeat the previous recipe. Use 1$^1/_2$ tablespoons of sesame paste, or 2 tablespoons of peanut butter mixed with 2 teaspoons of sesame oil, and blend the mixture with the soya sauce and peanut oil.

### Hot and Savoury Bean-Curd 'Pudding'
(for 6–8 portions)

This is a West China, Szechuan dish, called Ma-Po Tofu.

| | |
|---|---|
| 4 cakes bean-curd | 2 tablespoons soya sauce |
| 6 medium-size dried Chinese mushrooms | 1 teaspoon tofu cheese |
| | 1 tablespoon hoisin sauce |
| 1 medium-size green sweet pepper | 2 cloves garlic |
| | 1–2 teaspoons chilli sauce |
| 1–2 chilli peppers | 1 tablespoon tomato purée |
| 3 tablespoons vegetable oil | 1 teaspoon sugar |
| $^3/_4$ tablespoon salted black beans | 3 teaspoons cornflour |
| | 2 tablespoons butter |
| 2 teaspoons soya paste | 1 tablespoon sherry |

Cut each piece of bean-curd into a dozen pieces. Cut the pepper and chilli pepper in $^1/_4$-inch pieces, discarding seeds. Soak the black beans in a cup of water for 15 minutes, drain and mash. Soak the mushrooms in a cup of hot water for $^1/_2$ an hour. Drain, retain water, remove stalks and chop coarsely. Crush and chop the garlic.

Heat the oil in a frying-pan. Add the pepper, chilli pepper, mushroom and garlic, and stir-fry on a medium heat for 3–4 minutes. Add the butter and all the other seasoning and flavouring ingredients, and continue to stir-fry for another 3–4 minutes. Mix the cornflour with 4 tablespoons of mushroom water. Add to pan and stir quickly to blend with the other ingredients. Finally, pour in the bean-curd. Turn and stir it in the bubbling sauce, until it is well heated through, and all of it is well covered and mixed with the sauce. This dish is greatly appreciated by rice eaters.

For non-vegetarians, add $\frac{1}{4}$–$\frac{1}{2}$ lb of minced pork or chicken with the garlic, black beans and pepper to the initial stir-frying, and extend the cooking time by a couple of minutes.

### Hot and Pungent Bean-Curd Pudding

This is a variation of the previous recipe, in which three extra flavouring ingredients are added: $1\frac{1}{2}$ tablespoons chopped hot-pickled Szechuan cabbage, 2 tablespoons vinegar and $1\frac{1}{2}$ tablespoons Red-in-Snow pickled greens.

When the latter is chopped into coarse mince for sprinkling over the bean-curd just before serving, it changes dramatically the flavour and character of the dish. The Szechuan cabbage and the vinegar should be added at the beginning of the second stage of the stir-frying along with the butter.

### Red-cooked Bean-Curd with Bean-Curd Sticks
(6–8 portions)

Bean-curd sticks come in about 20-inch lengths. They have a glossy, lacquer-like surface, creamy in colour. They are hard and have to be soaked before using.

| | |
|---|---|
| 3 cakes bean-curd | 2 slices ginger root |
| 3 sticks bean-curd | 1 teaspoon soya paste |
| 6 medium-size dried Chinese mushrooms | $2\frac{1}{2}$ tablespoons soya sauce |
| | 1 teaspoon chilli sauce |

| | |
|---|---|
| 2 stalks 'golden needles' (lily bud stems) | 1 teaspoon sugar |
| | 1 tablespoon hoisin sauce |
| 1 stalk spring onion | 1 tablespoon butter |
| 2 tablespoons vegetable oil | ³/₄ pint Vegetable Broth |
| 2 tablespoons sherry | 1 tablespoon tomato purée |
| 2 cloves garlic | |

Cut each bean-curd cake into 6 pieces. Soak the 'golden needles' and bean-curd sticks for 1 hour in warm water. Drain and cut into 2-inch segments. Soak the dried mushrooms in a cup of water for ¹/₂ an hour. Drain, remove the stems, and cut each mushroom into halves or quarters, depending on size. Keep the water. Cut the spring onion into 1-inch segments. Crush the garlic and shred the ginger.

Heat the oil in a casserole. Add the garlic, ginger and ¹/₂ the spring onion. Stir-fry for ¹/₂ a minute. Add the mushrooms, 'golden needles' and bean-curd stick. Stir-fry together for 3 minutes. Add all the seasoning and flavouring ingredients, including the broth. Bring to the boil and simmer very gently for ¹/₂ an hour. Add 4–5 tablespoons of mushroom water and 1 tablespoon of sherry and mix them with the sauce until well blended. Add all the bean-curd pieces. Turn and mix them in the sauce and other ingredients. Cover and allow to simmer very gently for ¹/₄ of an hour. Sprinkle with the rest of the sherry and spring onion, and serve in the casserole.

For non-vegetarians, simply add ¹/₂–1 lb of red-cooked meat – pork or beef – to cook with the bean-curd during the last ¹/₂ an hour.


## STIR-FRIED BEAN-CURDS

Bean-curds can be stir-fried with almost any kind of vegetable which is traditionally stir-fried. When making such dishes it is customary to stir-fry the vegetables with ingredients which will produce a good quantity of sauce or gravy, which is in turn absorbed by the bean-curd during the final phase of stir-frying together, producing a highly savoury dish.

### Bean-Curd Stir-fried with Bean Sprouts (or Spinach)

3 cakes bean-curd
$^1/_2$ lb bean sprouts (or spinach)
3 large Chinese dried mushrooms
3 stalks spring onion
3 tablespoons vegetable oil
$1^1/_2$ tablespoons butter
2 cloves garlic
1 slice ginger root

1 teaspoon soya paste
2 tablespoons soya sauce
$^1/_2$ tablespoon hoisin sauce
1 teaspoon chilli sauce
1 teaspoon sugar
$^1/_2$ teaspoon vegetable bouillon powder
4 tablespoons Vegetable Broth
1 tablespoon sherry

Cut each bean-curd into 6–8 pieces. Cut the spring onion into 1-inch segments. Soak the mushrooms in $^1/_2$ cup of water for $^1/_2$ an hour, remove the stems, and shred into matchstick strips. Crush the garlic and shred the ginger.

Heat the oil in a frying-pan. Add garlic, ginger and $^1/_2$ the spring onion and stir-fry on a medium heat for $^1/_2$ a minute. Add the bean paste, mushrooms, soya sauce, hoisin sauce, chilli sauce, sugar, vegetable bouillon powder and Vegetable Broth. Stir-fry them together for 2 minutes. Add the bean-curd. Turn and stir in the sauce until well covered and heated through. Remove the bean-curd and put aside to keep hot. Add butter and sherry. Raise the heat to its highest. Pour the bean sprouts into the pan to mix and turn quickly in the bubbling sauce and oil for 2 minutes. Add the remaining spring onion, and return the bean-curd to the pan. Turn and stir the contents for 1 minute and serve. Eat immediately as the 'heat effect' is an important part of the dish's flavour. If spinach is used instead of bean sprouts, only the tender leaves should be chosen, and the amount of butter should be increased by 1 tablespoon.

## Bean-Curd Stir-fried with French Beans

Repeat the previous recipe, using French beans instead of bean sprouts. The beans must be topped and tailed and parboiled for 3–4 minutes before they are fried, and the stir-frying prolonged by about 1 minute, before the bean-curd is returned to the pan for the final stir-frying.

In either of the above two recipes the bean-curd can also be simply stir-fried once, placed at the centre of a hot serving dish, and later surrounded by the vegetables when they too have been stir-fried. In such cases, the stir-frying of the bean-curd will have to be prolonged by 1 minute. In other instances, the bean-curd can be deep-fried first for 2 minutes and drained, before it is stir-fried. How it is cooked at this stage is a matter of taste and inclination.

For non-vegetarians, $^1/_4$–$^1/_2$ lb of minced pork is usually added to the initial stir-frying, which is prolonged by a couple of minutes. The amounts of all the seasonings and flavourers employed are increased by one-quarter. For more elaborate dishes, shrimps and crab eggs or crab meat can be used instead of minced pork or in conjunction with it, in the initial stir-frying.

## Deep-fried Bean-Curd Stir-fried with Duck Eggs and Cucumber Skins
### (for 4–6 portions)

| | |
|---|---|
| 3 cakes bean-curd | pepper (to taste) |
| 3 duck eggs (hard boiled) | 2 tablespoons vegetable oil |
| 6-inch segment cucumber | 2 tablespoons sherry |
| oil for deep-frying | 2 tablespoons butter |
| 1 clove garlic | $^1/_2$ tablespoon soya sauce |

| 4 tablespoons Vegetable | 1 tablespoon light soya sauce |
|---|---|
| Broth | $^1/_2$ tablespoon hoisin sauce |
| 1 medium-size onion | $^1/_2$ teaspoon sugar |
| 2 teaspoons tofu cheese | 2 teaspoons vinegar |

Cut each bean-curd into 6–8 pieces. Deep-fry for 2 minutes and drain. Chop the duck eggs coarsely. Cut the cucumber into 3 equal segments. Slice each segment vertically lengthwise into 8 pieces, each piece having some green skin. Cut the onion into very thin slices. Crush the garlic.

Heat 3 tablespoons of oil in a frying-pan. Add the garlic and onion. Stir-fry for $1^1/_2$ minutes. Add the eggs, light soya sauce, broth, pepper to taste and sherry. Turn and stir for $^1/_2$ a minute. Add the bean-curd. Mix and stir the pieces for 2 minutes with the egg and sauce. Pour them out on to the centre of a well-heated serving dish.

Heat the butter in a separate frying-pan. Pour in the cucumber. Add the soya sauce, hoisin sauce, sugar and vinegar. Stir-fry for $1^1/_2$ minutes. Spoon the cucumber around the bean-curd and duck eggs at the centre of the dish, and serve.

### Deep-fried Bean-Curd Stir-fried with Eggs, Mushrooms and 'Wood Ears'
(for 4–6 portions)

| 3 cakes bean-curd | 1 teaspoon sugar |
|---|---|
| 3 eggs | $^1/_4$ teaspoon vegetable |
| 4 medium-size dried Chinese | bouillon powder |
| mushrooms | 4 tablespoons Vegetable |
| 2 tablespoons 'wood ears' | Broth |
| fungi | 3 tablespoons mushroom |
| 2 stalks spring onion | water |
| 3 tablespoons vegetable oil | 2 tablespoons sherry |
| 2 tablespoons butter | $^1/_2$ teaspoon salt |
| $1^1/_2$ tablespoons soya sauce | pepper (to taste) |

$^1/_2$ tablespoon hoisin sauce     $^1/_2$ tablespoon sesame oil

Cut each piece of bean-curd cake into 6 pieces. Beat the eggs lightly for 10 seconds. Soak the mushrooms in a cup of warm water for $^1/_2$ an hour. Remove the stems, shred the mushrooms into strips, and retain the water. Soak the 'wood ears' for $^1/_2$ an hour, rinse and clean thoroughly. Cut the spring onion into 1-inch segments. Deep-fry the bean-curd for 2–3 minutes and drain.

Heat the oil in a frying-pan. Add the mushrooms and 'wood ears' and stir-fry for 1 minute on a medium heat. Add the soya sauce, hoisin sauce, sugar, vegetable bouillon powder, broth and 3 tablespoons of mushroom water. Continue to heat and stir for 2 minutes. Add the pieces of bean-curd. Turn them to mix with the mushroom and 'wood ears' for 2 minutes until well covered with sauce.

In another frying-pan, melt the butter on a medium heat, add the spring onion and pour in the beaten egg. Tilt and shake the pan so that the egg covers the bottom of the pan evenly. As soon as the egg has set, break it up into $^1/_2$-inch pieces. Sprinkle with the salt and pepper. Pour in the sherry. Turn the egg over once, and pour it into the pan containing the bean-curd, mushrooms and 'wood ears'. Turn and mix them once together over medium heat, pour the contents on to a serving dish, sprinkle with sesame oil and serve. Not only is this dish aromatic, the combination of the black of the mushrooms and 'wood ears' with the yellow of the egg, the green of the onion and brown of the bean-curd, make an appealing array of colours.

In its non-vegetarian form, $^1/_4$–$^1/_2$ lb of thinly sliced lean pork is stir-fried in oil for a couple of minutes before the mushrooms and 'wood ears' are added. After 3–4 minutes of cooking together with slightly increased quantities of seasonings and flavourers, and later with bean-curd added, the contents combined with the stir-fried eggs are made aromatic by the last-moment addition of sesame oil and sherry. In fact, this is a well-known Peking dish called Mu Shu Jou. In the South, even greater savouriness is achieved by adding 2–3 oz of oysters or mussels into the stir-frying with the pork.

### Stir-fried Shredded Bean-Curd with Dried Bamboo-shoots, Dried Mushrooms and 'Golden Needles' and Seaweed ('hair type')
#### (for 5–6 portions)

3 cakes bean-curd
2 stalks spring onion
3 oz Chinese dried mushrooms
3 oz Chinese dried bamboo-shoots
2 stalks 'golden needles' (lily bud stems)
2 tablespoons vegetable oil
1 tablespoon butter
1 tablespoon light soya sauce
1 teaspoon tofu cheese
2 tablespoons Clear-simmer Broth (page 73)
3 oz seaweed ('hair type' but optional)

1¹/₂ tablespoons vegetable oil
1 tablespoon sesame oil
1 tablespoon soya sauce
¹/₂ tablespoon hoisin sauce
¹/₄ teaspoon vegetable bouillon powder
6 tablespoons Vegetable Broth
2 tablespoons sherry
1¹/₂ teaspoons cornflour blended in 2 tablespoons mushroom water
¹/₂ teaspoon sugar
1 teaspoon chilli sauce

Cut the bean-curd into ¹/₄-inch-wide strips the length of a matchstick. Cut the spring onion and 'golden needles' into 2-inch segments. Soak the 'golden needles' in warm water for 1 hour and drain. Soak the dried bamboo-shoots and mushrooms in warm water, the former for 1 hour and the latter for ¹/₂ an hour. Shred into matchstick strips, removing stalks. Soak the seaweed for 1 hour with two changes of water. Rub with 2

teaspoons of oil and 2 teaspoons of sherry, and leave to stand
for $^1/_2$ an hour.

Heat 2 tablespoons of oil and butter in a frying-pan. Add the
'golden needles' to stir-fry on a medium heat for 2 minutes.
Add the spring onion, tofu cheese, light soya sauce and Clear-
simmer Broth. Continue to stir-fry for 1 minute. Add the bean-
curd strips, turn them in the sauce to mix with the 'golden
needles' and spring onion and simmer gently for another 2
minutes.

In another pan, heat $1^1/_2$ tablespoons of oil with sesame oil.
Add the shredded dried bamboo-shoots, shredded mushrooms and seaweed. Stir-fry them for 2 minutes. Add all the
seasonings and flavourers, including the Vegetable Broth and
sherry. Stir-fry them together for 2 minutes. Finally, add the
cornflour/mushroom water mixture and continue to stir-fry
for 2 minutes. Pour the contents of one pan into the other. Toss
and turn them until the strips are evenly mixed.

Pour the contents neatly on to a heatproof serving dish.
Place the dish in a steamer and steam for 15 minutes and serve.


## CLEAR-SIMMERED BEAN-CURDS

Bean-curds are traditionally cooked in China either with a very
savoury sauce (as illustrated in the previous recipes) or by
simmering them in a clear broth with not more than one or two
vegetable ingredients. This produces a dish which is distinctive for its purity and its undisguised presentation of the
native flavours of the principal ingredients. It provides a welcome contrast to the majority of the other dishes on the table.

## Clear-simmered Bean-Curd with Lettuce and Transparent Noodles
### (for 6–8 portions)

4 cakes bean-curd
$^1/_2$ lb lettuce
$1^1/_2$ pints Clear-simmer Broth
  (see page 73)
1 teaspoon salt
1 tablespoon light soya sauce

2 oz transparent noodles
  (before soaking)
1 teaspoon vegetable
  bouillon powder
pepper (to taste)
1 teaspoon sesame oil

Cut each piece of bean-curd into quarters. Clean the lettuce thoroughly, discarding any discoloured leaves, and cut away the root and tougher parts of the stem. Cut each leaf in half slantwise across the stem. Soak the noodles in water for 10 minutes and drain.

Place the lettuce and bean-curd, together with all other ingredients and broth in a heatproof bowl to steam for $^1/_2$ an hour, and serve.

## Clear-simmered Bean-Curd with Bean Sprouts, Water Chestnuts and Sliced Cucumbers
### (for 6–8 portions)

4 cakes bean-curd
$^1/_4$ lb fat bean sprouts
$^1/_2$ medium-size cucumber
3 water chestnuts
$1^1/_2$ pints Clear-simmer Broth
  (see page 73)

1 teaspoon salt
1 tablespoon light soya sauce
1 teaspoon vegetable
  bouillon powder
pepper (to taste)
1 teaspoon sesame oil

Cut each piece of bean-curd into quarters. Thoroughly rinse and wash the bean sprouts, which must be very fresh. Cut the cucumber lengthwise into double mahjong-sized pieces (approximately 2 × 1 × $^1/_2$ inch), each piece backed by skin,

which should be lightly scraped. Cut each water chestnut into
4–6 slices.

Place all the ingredients in a heatproof bowl, pouring the
broth on top. Place the bowl in a steamer and steam for $1/2$ an
hour. Serve in the bowl.

For non-vegetarians, add 1 tablespoon of dried shrimps parboiled for 2 minutes and 2 tablespoons of fresh shrimps. A
slice or two of ginger root and a tablespoon of sherry are useful
in suppressing a too-strong fishiness in the dish.

Before we conclude this section on tofu or bean-curd, it is
worth noting that during elaborate Buddhist banquets, where
imitation poultry, fish and meats are served, often looking very
like the real thing, the basic material used in such craftsmanship is always bean-curd with bean-curd skin and bean-curd
sticks. The usual meat dishes which are simulated in vegetarian food are the red-cooked ones, as the bean-curd and its
by-products, when braised or fried with soya sauce and soya
paste, becomes almost precisely the same colour as meat, fish
or poultry when similarly cooked. Bean-curd skin also, when
used in layers, has the appearance and texture of the flaking
flesh of fish or poultry which had been marinaded and deep-
fried, whilst the white meat of chicken or the under-layer flesh
of fish or pork, which had not been touched by soya, can be
imitated by the creamy softness of uncoloured bean-curd, or
bean-curd skins used in layers. The legs, claws and crest of
birds, and the tails of fish can be made from bean-curd sticks
cut and shaped with scissors after soaking. Such reconstruc-
tions of birds, fish and meat are marvelled at by the diners.
Endeavours like these, however, border more on handicrafts
than cooking and since any effort at a like perfection would
take days or weeks of patient craftsmanship, I would not
recommend the average cook to try them. This is an area best
left to the monks in their cells or in their vast open-plan kitchens, where work starts at about 3 a.m. and where thought is
directed rather towards achieving perfection than cooking the

family's meal. For we who are more materially grounded, it is best to direct our energy into areas where maximum results can be achieved with minimum effort, even though we are dealing with a type of cooking whose traditions and techniques are derived in the main from a more leisured past.

# Chinese Salads

Although we Chinese seldom eat anything raw, and our cuisine has no great salad tradition, there are a number of salad dishes which are by no means uninteresting, and which can be produced in the modern kitchen and used to supplement the usual Western range of salads.

For non-vegetarians in China, shredded roast duck or chicken meat and a few teaspoons of shrimp oil are often added to any of the following salads.

No portions are given for salads as they can be served either as a main or a side dish.

## Chinese Carrot Salad

| | |
|---|---|
| 1½ lb young carrots | 2 tablespoons vinegar |
| 3 teaspoons salt | 1 tablespoon sugar |
| 2 tablespoons soya sauce | 1 tablespoon sesame oil |

Scrape and clean the carrots thoroughly. Slice them diagonally into very thin slices. Cut each slice again into six strips. Parboil the carrots for 2 minutes and drain. When drained, sprinkle and rub salt thoroughly into the carrot strips. Leave them to stand for 1½ hours, and pour away all the water which has been extracted by the salt. Give them one quick rinse under running water and drain and dry on absorbent paper.

Place the carrot strips in a salad bowl. Sprinkle with sugar, soya sauce, vinegar and sesame oil. Toss them together a few times and serve either on their own or with other ingredients in a mixed salad.

## Cabbage and Celery Mustard Salad

In China we would normally use Chinese cabbage for this salad. In the West, where Chinese cabbage is not always available, it might be best to use a mixture of Savoy cabbage and celery or lettuce.

| | |
|---|---|
| 1 lb young Savoy cabbage | 1 tablespoon wine vinegar |
| $^3/_4$ lb celery (or lettuce) | 1 teaspoon chilli sauce |
| $1^1/_2$ tablespoons mustard powder | 1 tablespoon sherry |
| | $1^1/_2$ tablespoons vegetable oil |
| 2 tablespoons soya sauce | 1 tablespoon sesame oil |
| $^1/_2$ teaspoon salt | |

Clean the vegetables thoroughly, break into individual leaves or stems. Cut away the roots and unsightly parts. Cut the celery diagonally into 2-inch pieces, and the cabbage similarly. Plunge them into a large pan of boiling water to parboil for 3 minutes. Drain and place in a casserole. Mix the mustard in a bowl with an appropriate amount of water (2–3 tablespoons), stir into a paste, add the oils, soya sauce, salt, vinegar, chilli sauce and sherry. Stir until well blended.

Whilst the vegetables in the casserole are still hot, spoon the mustard mixture from the bowl evenly over them. Toss and stir them together until they are well mixed. Turn the heat on under the casserole and close the lid. Heat for 1 minute. Turn off the heat and leave in a cool place to cool. When cold, serve either in the casserole or in a normal salad bowl.

## 'Chinese Salad'

| | |
|---|---|
| $1^1/_2$ lb Cos lettuce | $^1/_2$ teaspoon salt |
| $^1/_4$ lb young carrots | 3 tablespoons vegetable oil |
| 4 medium-size tomatoes (must be fresh and firm) | 2 tablespoons Vegetable Broth |
| 1 medium-size onion | 2 slices ginger root |

$^1/_2$ lb bean sprouts (must be
  fresh and fat)
$^3/_4$ tablespoons chopped
  chives
3 cloves garlic

$^1/_2$ teaspoon vegetable
  bouillon powder
2 tablespoons soya sauce
1 tablespoon hoisin sauce
$1^1/_2$ tablespoons sherry
1 tablespoon sesame oil

Clean the lettuce, cut away the roots, and further cut or tear
the leaves into 2–3-inch pieces. Slice the carrots into matchstick
strips. Skin the tomatoes and cut each one into quarters. Wash
and rinse the bean sprouts and drain thoroughly. Chop the
chives and onion coarsely. Crush the garlic, shred the ginger,
and chop both into coarse grains. Heat the oil in a small pan.
When hot add the onion, garlic and ginger. Stir-fry for 1
minute. Add the broth and vegetable bouillon powder. Stir
around 2 or 3 times and turn off the heat. Mix the soya sauce,
hoisin sauce, salt, sherry and sesame oil in a bowl. Pour the
contents of the pan into the bowl and mix all ingredients
together until well blended.

Place the vegetables in a salad bowl. Sprinkle the contents of
the other bowl over them. Toss until well mixed. Sprinkle the
chives over them and serve.

### Bean Sprout and Bamboo-shoot Salad

8 oz bamboo-shoots
4 oz braised bamboo-shoots
  (canned)
1 lb fat bean sprouts (must be
  fresh)
2 stalks spring onion
3 slices ginger root
2 cloves garlic
1 teaspoon vegetable
  bouillon powder

2 tablespoons Vegetable
  Broth
2 tablespoons soya sauce
$^3/_4$ tablespoon hoisin sauce
1 teaspoon chilli oil
1 tablespoon sherry
2 tablespoons vegetable oil
$^3/_4$ tablespoon sesame oil

Slice both types of bamboo-shoots into strips the length of a matchstick and twice as wide. Wash and rinse the bean sprouts, parboil for 2 minutes, and drain thoroughly. Parboil the bamboo-shoots (not the braised type) for 4 minutes and drain. Chop the spring onion into $1/6$-inch pieces. Shred the ginger, crush the garlic and chop both coarsely. Place them in a bowl and add all the other seasoning and flavouring ingredients. Mix until well blended.

Place the bamboo-shoots and bean sprouts in a salad bowl. Sprinkle the blended mixture from the other bowl evenly over them. Toss and serve.

### Asparagus, Bamboo-shoot and Cucumber Salad

| | |
|---|---|
| 1 bunch asparagus | $1/4$ teaspoon vegetable |
| 6-inch segment of a medium- | bouillon powder |
| size cucumber | 1 teaspoon chilli sauce |
| 6 oz bamboo-shoots | $1^1/2$ tablespoons Vegetable |
| 2 tablespoons soya sauce | Oil |
| 1 tablespoon hoisin sauce | $3/4$ tablespoon sesame oil |
| 2 tablespoons Vegetable | 2 tablespoons sherry |
| Broth | |

Remove the root and tougher end of the asparagus. Halve each remaining piece lengthwise. Cut again into 3-inch segments. Parboil for 4–5 minutes and drain completely. Cut the bamboo-shoots into similar sized pieces. Parboil for 5–6 minutes and drain. Cut the cucumber into half lengthwise and then again into similar length slivers.

Mix all the seasoning and flavouring ingredients in a bowl until well blended.

Place the three vegetables in a salad bowl. Pour the blended mixture in the other bowl over them. Toss and leave to chill for 30 minutes in a refrigerator and serve.

## The 'Three Fairy' Salad

1½ lb Chinese cabbage (or lettuce)
4 oz radish
2 tablespoons coriander leaves (coarsely chopped)

1½ tablespoons salt
1 medium onion
2 chilli peppers
3 tablespoons vegetable oil
3 teaspoons sesame oil

Clean the cabbage thoroughly, remove the root, and cut the leaves into approximately 1½–2-inch pieces. Chop the radish and mix it with the cabbage. Sprinkle salt over them and work it gently into the vegetables. Leave to season for 3 hours. Sprinkle with 1 cupful of water. Drain, and dry vegetables thoroughly on absorbent paper. Slice the onion into thin slices. Chop the pepper, discarding the seeds.

Heat the oil in a small frying-pan. Stir-fry the onion and pepper on a medium heat for 3 minutes, then discard them. Add the sesame oil to the remaining oil in the pan.

Sprinkle the blended oil over the radish and cabbage. Toss and sprinkle with chopped coriander and serve.


## The 'Eight Precious' Salad

1 bowl shredded carrots
1 bowl bean sprouts
¼ bowl 'golden needles' (lily bud stems) (soaked)
¼ bowl 'wood ears' fungi (soaked)
¼ bowl shredded turnips
6 tablespoons vegetable oil
1 tablespoon sesame oil
½ teaspoon salt
2 tablespoons soya sauce
½ tablespoon hoisin sauce

½ bowl shredded bamboo-shoots
¼ bowl shredded tofu skin (soaked)
¼ bowl Chinese dried mushrooms (soaked)
1½ tablespoons vinegar
½ teaspoon vegetable bouillon powder
2 tablespoons Vegetable Broth

Soak the 'wood ears' and mushrooms for $^1/_2$ an hour. Cut the mushrooms into strips and rinse and clean the 'ears' thoroughly. Soak the 'golden needles' and bean-curd skin in warm water for 2 hours and drain. Cut both into approximately 2-inch segments.

Heat 3 tablespoons of oil in a saucepan. Add the carrots and turnips to stir-fry together for 3 minutes. Add the sprouts and bamboo-shoots and continue to stir-fry for 2 minutes.

Heat the other 3 tablespoons of oil in another saucepan. Add the 'needles', mushrooms and bean-curd skin and stir-fry them together for 3 minutes. Add the 'wood ears' and continue to stir-fry for 2 minutes. Mix the broth with the sesame oil and all the other seasoning and flavouring ingredients in a separate bowl.

Mix the two lots of stir-fried vegetables in a large salad bowl. Sprinkle with the blended mixture from the other bowl. Toss and serve hot or cold.

Serve with plenty of plain boiled or steamed rice. If desired, add some finely chopped hot-pickled Szechuan cabbage or Red-in-Snow pickled greens, and decorate with radishes and baby tomatoes. A few finely chopped slices of ginger root can also be added if liked.

Shredded lettuce and Chinese cabbage are often added to this salad: there are many variations. If not available, the bamboo-shoots and 'golden needles' can be omitted.

# Chinese Hot Salads

As the name suggests, a hot salad differs from an ordinary one in that it is served and eaten hot. The essence of such dishes is fresh crispness combined with heat, achieved by tossing the main vegetables briefly in hot oil and flavouring ingredients and sauces. Indeed, in some instances the hot oil and flavouring ingredients and sauces enhance the original flavours of the raw vegetables. The process of preparing these hot salads is essentially stir-frying, but it is even swifter than ordinary quick stir-frying. An integral part of the Chinese way of preparing vegetables, it can prove a very useful addition to the average Western kitchen.

### Hot Sweet Pepper and Bamboo-shoot Salad

2 large red sweet peppers
2 large green sweet peppers
5–6 oz bamboo-shoots
3–4 oz soya-braised bamboo-shoots (usually available canned)

2 tablespoons corn oil
$1^1/_2$ tablespoons butter
$1^1/_2$ tablespoons sesame oil

#### FLAVOURING INGREDIENTS

2 tablespoons soya sauce
1 tablespoon hoisin sauce
$1^1/_2$ tablespoons sherry
2 teaspoons sugar

$^1/_2$ teaspoon vegetable bouillon powder
$1^1/_2$ teaspoons chilli sauce

Chop the peppers and bamboo-shoots into matchstick strips. Mix the flavouring ingredients in a separate bowl.

Heat the oil, butter and sesame oil in a large saucepan or frying-pan. When it is very hot, turn and toss the shredded vegetables in the oil for $1/2$ a minute. Pour the flavouring ingredients evenly over the vegetables. Continue to turn and toss and stir-fry for $1/2$ a minute. Serve on a well-heated serving dish and eat immediately. The rapid turning and tossing of the vegetables in hot oil creates a very bright flavoursome and aromatic dish.

## Hot Bean Sprouts, Bamboo-shoots and Mushroom Salad

| | |
|---|---|
| 1 lb fresh bean sprouts | 2 stalks spring onion |
| 4 oz bamboo-shoots | 2 tablespoons corn oil |
| 2 oz dried Chinese | $1^1/_2$ tablespoons butter |
|   mushrooms | 1 tablespoon sesame oil |

### FLAVOURING INGREDIENTS

| | |
|---|---|
| 2 tablespoons soya sauce | $1^1/_2$ teaspoons sugar |
| $3/_4$ tablespoon vegetable | 2 tablespoons dry sherry |
|   bouillon powder | 2 teaspoons mustard |

Soak the dried mushrooms for $1/2$ an hour. Discard the stems and shred the mushrooms into matchstick strips. Shred the bamboo-shoots in the same way. Cut the spring onion (including the green parts) into $2^1/_2$-inch pieces. Mix the flavouring ingredients in a bowl.

Heat the oil, butter and sesame oil in a large saucepan or frying-pan. When it is very hot add the mushrooms. Stir-fry them over high heat for 15 seconds. Add all the other shredded vegetables. Continue to stir-fry rapidly for $1/2$ a minute. Pour the flavouring ingredients evenly over the vegetables. Stir-fry for a further $1/2$ a minute, and serve on a well-heated serving dish.

## Hot Spinach and Bamboo-shoot Salad

1¹/₂ lb fresh leaf spinach
¹/₂ lb bamboo-shoots
  (canned)

3 tablespoons corn oil
1¹/₂ tablespoons butter
1 tablespoon sesame oil

### FLAVOURING INGREDIENTS

2¹/₂ tablespoons soya sauce
1¹/₂ teaspoons sugar

salt and pepper (to taste)

Clean the spinach thoroughly. Cut away and discard all the coarser stems and leaves. Cut the bamboo-shoots into ¹/₄-inch-thick strips.

Heat the butter in a small frying-pan on a medium heat. Add the bamboo-shoots. Sprinkle them with salt and pepper (to taste) and stir-fry them for ¹/₂ a minute. Heat the oil in a large saucepan until it is very hot. Add the spinach and turn it rapidly in the oil for ³/₄ of a minute over high heat. Sprinkle the soya sauce and sugar evenly over the spinach and continue to stir-fry for a further ¹/₄ of a minute. Add the buttered bamboo-shoots and sesame oil to the spinach. Stir-fry the two vegetables together, still over a high heat, for a further ¹/₂ a minute and serve.

The dark green of the spinach and ivory whiteness of the bamboo-shoots make an attractive contrast in colour as well as in texture.

## Hot Mushrooms and Asparagus Salad

1 lb fresh mushrooms
¹/₄ lb Chinese dried
  mushrooms
1 bundle asparagus

2 tablespoons corn oil
2 tablespoons butter
1 tablespoon sesame oil

$1^1/_2$ tablespoons soya sauce

1 tablespoon soya paste (if
   available)

1 tablespoon hoisin sauce

2 tablespoons dry sherry

1 teaspoon sugar

Remove the tougher ends of the asparagus. Chop the rest into pieces $^1/_4$–$^1/_2$-inch thick. Parboil for 3 minutes in a big pan of boiling water. Strain the water; add the butter and toss over a medium heat for $1^1/_2$ minutes. Soak the Chinese dried mushrooms for $^1/_2$ an hour in a cupful of warm water. Retain 3 tablespoons of this water, discard the stems and slice the mushrooms into $^1/_4$-inch-thick strips. Discard the stems of the fresh mushrooms and slice them into strips of a similar size. Heat the oil and sesame oil in a saucepan. When hot, add both types of mushrooms and stir-fry them together for 1 minute over a high heat. Add the butter, asparagus and all the flavouring ingredients. Continue to stir-fry and toss for $^1/_2$ a minute and serve.

## Hot Cabbage, Carrots and Radish Salad

1 lb white cabbage

$^1/_2$ lb young carrots

3 large radishes

3–4 teaspoons salt

2 tablespoons corn oil

2 tablespoons butter

1 tablespoon soya sauce

2 teaspoons sugar

$1^1/_2$ tablespoons wine
   vinegar

1 tablespoon sherry

2 teaspoons mustard powder

Shred all three vegetables into $^1/_4$-inch-thick strips. Sprinkle and rub with salt, and leave to season for 2 hours. Drain away any water. Mix the flavouring ingredients in a bowl.

Heat the oil and butter in a large saucepan. When very hot, add all the shredded vegetables, and stir-fry over high heat for

1 minute. Add the flavouring ingredients, continue to toss and stir-fry for a further minute, and serve.

## Hot Lettuce and Cabbage Salad with Sweet and Sour Sauce

1 lb white cabbage or
  Chinese cabbage
1 head Cos lettuce or leaf
  lettuce
2 tablespoons corn oil

1 tablespoon butter
1 tablespoon sesame oil
5–8 tablespoons Sweet and
  Sour Sauce (see page 81)

Remove the roots of the vegetables. Cut each leaf slantwise into 2 or 3 pieces. Prepare the Sweet and Sour Sauce, and keep warm in a small pan.

Heat the oil, sesame oil and butter in a large saucepan. When hot, add the cabbage and turn and stir-fry over a high heat for 1$^1$/$_2$ minutes. Add the lettuce and stir-fry the two vegetables together for $^1$/$_2$ a minute. Pour the Sweet and Sour Sauce over the vegetables. Turn and toss them in the sauce for a further 25 seconds and serve.

## Celery and Cucumber Salad with Beetroot

1 head celery (about $^3$/$_4$ lb)
1 medium-size cucumber

$^1$/$_4$–$^1$/$_2$ lb cooked beetroot

### FLAVOURING INGREDIENTS

1$^1$/$_2$ tablespoons soya sauce
1 tablespoon hoisin sauce
2 teaspoons sugar
1 tablespoon wine vinegar
1 tablespoon dry sherry

1$^1$/$_2$ teaspoons chilli sauce
2 tablespoons corn oil (or
  peanut oil)
1 tablespoon butter
1 tablespoon sesame oil

Trim the beetroot and cut into $^1$/$_4$-inch-thick strips. Clean the cucumber and celery thoroughly, and slice into similar size strips (retaining all the skin of the cucumber). Mix and toss the three types of vegetable together. Mix the flavouring ingredients in a bowl.

Heat the butter and oils in a large saucepan or frying-pan. When very hot, add all the vegetables and stir-fry rapidly over a high heat for 1 minute. Sprinkle the flavouring ingredients evenly over the vegetables, and continue to toss, turn and stir-fry for 1 minute, then serve.


### Chinese Egg, Mushrooms and Spring Onion Hot Salad

3 eggs
$^1/_2$ lb mushrooms
5–6 stalks spring onion
2 tablespoons butter
$1^1/_2$ tablespoons vegetable oil
  (corn or peanut)

$1^1/_2$ tablespoons sesame oil
$^1/_2$ teaspoon salt
pepper (to taste)

#### FLAVOURING INGREDIENTS

$1^1/_2$ tablespoons soya sauce
$^1/_4$ teaspoon vegetable
  bouillon powder

1 teaspoon chilli sauce
2 tablespoons dry sherry
$1^1/_2$ teaspoons sugar

Beat the egg lightly with the salt and pepper. Melt the butter in a frying-pan. Make a very thin omelette with the beaten egg. When the omelette is cool, slice into very thin strips (double the length of matchsticks or longer). Wash and rinse the mushrooms thoroughly, remove the stems and slice into thin strips. Chop the spring onion into $2^1/_2$-inch segments.

Heat the butter and oils in a large frying-pan or saucepan. When hot add the shredded mushrooms. Toss and stir-fry for $^1/_2$ a minute on a high heat. Add the spring onion and shredded omelette, stir-fry and turn for $^1/_2$ a minute. Sprinkle the flavouring ingredients evenly over the contents of the pan. Toss, turn and stir-fry for a further $^1/_2$ a minute, then serve.

## Chinese Hot Rice Salad

1 lb cooked rice (boiled)
3 soya eggs
1/4 lb frozen green peas
1/4 lb small button
  mushrooms
3–4 oz Chinese salted green
  pickles (or use 1 small can
  soya-braised bamboo-
  shoots – available from
  most Chinese food stores)

2–3 leaves crispy lettuce
2 tablespoons butter
2 1/2 tablespoons vegetable oil
3 stalks spring onion

### FLAVOURING INGREDIENTS

salt and pepper (to taste)    1 tablespoon light soya sauce

Prepare the soya eggs by simmering hard-boiled eggs in soya sauce for 10–15 minutes (see page 124). Leave to cool in the sauce. When cold, dice the brown eggs in 1/4-inch cubes. Chop the pickles and spring onion coarsely. Drain the water from the mushrooms. Thaw the peas.

    Heat the oil and butter in a large saucepan. When hot, add the mushrooms, pickles and green peas. Stir-fry them together on a medium heat for 1/2 a minute. Add the lettuce and rice. Mix together and stir-fry for 1 1/2 minutes. Sprinkle the ingredients in the pan with salt, pepper and chopped eggs. Continue to stir-fry, turn and toss for 1 1/2 minutes on a medium heat. Serve in a well-heated bowl.

## Chinese Sweet Rice Salad

1 lb cooked rice
1/4 lb raisins
3-inch segment of cucumber
2–3 oz cooked beetroot

1–2 oranges or large
  mandarins
3 1/2 tablespoons vegetable oil
1 tablespoon sesame oil

4–5 oz cherries (or seedless
  grapes)

2 tablespoons soya sauce

4 teaspoons sugar

1$^{1}/_{2}$ tablespoons sherry

$^{1}/_{4}$ tablespoon vegetable
  bouillon powder

1$^{1}/_{2}$ tablespoons honey

2 tablespoons water

Trim the beetroot and dice into $^{1}/_{4}$-inch cubes. Dice the cucumber into similar size cubes, retaining the green skin. Remove the stones or pips of the cherries or grapes. Peel the oranges and chop them into small pieces. Mix the flavouring ingredients in a bowl.

Heat the oil and sesame oil in a large saucepan on a medium heat. Add the beetroot, cucumber and raisins. Turn them in the oil for $^{1}/_{4}$ of a minute. Add the rice and turn and toss in the oil and other ingredients for 1 minute. Add the grapes or cherries and oranges. Sprinkle the contents evenly with the flavouring ingredients. Stir-fry, turn and toss for 1$^{1}/_{2}$ more minutes and serve hot or cold.

# Sweets

Chinese cuisine is not particularly well known for its sweets, but there is a surprisingly large range of them. I am including a few sweet recipes here as sweet dishes are usually welcome after a succession of highly savoury dishes. As they are also used to break the sequence of savoury dishes, Chinese desserts are often served in the middle of a meal, sometimes in the form of a sweet soup.

### Sweet Steamed Buns

The process of making Sweet Steamed Buns is the same as making Savoury Steamed Buns (see page 122). The only difference lies in the stuffing. The favourite and most common Chinese sweet stuffings are sweet red bean paste and sesame seeds stir-fried with brown sugar. Sweet red bean paste can be purchased from Chinese provision shops. Half a pound of this paste or an equal amount of sesame seeds mixed with brown sugar should be stir-fried in $1^1/_2$ tablespoons of vegetable oil and $1^1/_2$ tablespoons of butter for 4–5 minutes on a low heat, and left to cool before being used as stuffing.

If sweet bean paste cannot be bought, it can be made by gently boiling 1 lb of red beans in 3 pints of water for $2^1/_2$ hours, stirring until all the husks float up. Remove the husks and filter through cheesecloth. Squeeze the beans in the cloth until they are nearly dry. Heat them with 1 tablespoon of sesame oil, 3 tablespoons of butter and 4–6 tablespoons of brown sugar on a gentle heat. Stir continually with a wooden spoon until the mixture is smooth and even (about 6–7 minutes).

Sweet sesame paste can be made by heating $^2/_3$ lb of sesame seeds with 5–6 tablespoons of brown sugar, 3–4 tablespoons of water, $1^1/_2$ tablespoons of sesame oil, $1^1/_2$ tablespoons of vegetable oil and 2 tablespoons of butter over a very gentle heat for 8–9 minutes, stirring constantly until the mixture is smooth. This paste and the sweet bean paste are the two basic stuffings used in Chinese desserts. At festival times these Sweet Steamed Buns are tipped with red vegetable colouring and displayed on tables in mountainous heaps for the children to pick up and eat.

### Sweet Orange 'Tea'
(for 4–6 portions)

Quite a few Chinese sweets occur in 'soup' form, which, although slightly strange to the Western palate, make a refreshing change in a large Chinese meal with a succession of savoury courses. This is one of them:

| | |
|---|---|
| 4–5 oranges | 1 tablespoon cornflour |
| 4 tablespoons sugar | $1^1/_2$ pints water |

Cut the oranges into halves and squeeze the juice from them. Add the sugar and cornflour to the water in a saucepan. Bring to the boil, stirring steadily. Add the orange juice to heat through. Serve in a large bowl placed in the centre of the table, or in small individual bowls. Good hot or chilled. (For variation, stir in 1 or 2 tablespoons of honey.)

### Sweet Pineapple and Cherry 'Tea'

Repeat the previous recipe, using a small can of pineapple and $^1/_2$ lb of fresh stoned cherries, heating them together with cornflour, sugar or honey and water for 5 minutes. Serve in a large bowl or divide the cherries, pineapple and hot sugared soup into small individual bowls.

## Sweet Almond 'Tea'
(for 4–6 portions)

In contrast to the two previous 'teas' which are clear 'soups', this is a thick one.

$^1/_2$ lb peeled almonds (or use 6 tablespoons almond paste or ground almond)
4 tablespoons rice flour

4 tablespoons sugar
1 teaspoon almond extract
$1^1/_2$ pints water
1 cup evaporated milk

Add the almond, flour and sugar to the water in a heavy saucepan. Bring to the boil and reduce the heat to the minimum. Continue to heat, stirring occasionally, for $^1/_4$ of an hour. Add the evaporated milk and almond extract. Stir and serve as soon as the liquid reboils, in small individual bowls.

## Almond Junket
(for 4–6 portions)

$^1/_4$ lb peeled almonds (or 3 tablespoons ground almond)
4 tablespoons sugar

1 teaspoon almond extract
2 packets gelatine
$^3/_4$ pint water
1 can evaporated milk

Grind the almond in a liquidizer into a fine powder. Heat half the amount of water and dissolve the gelatine in it.

Bring the rest of the water to the boil in a saucepan. Add the almond and dissolved gelatine. Heat gently and stir for 5–6 minutes. Pour in the evaporated milk and almond extract. Heat until the mixture is about to reboil. Stir and remove from heat to cool. When somewhat cool, pour into a flat dish or pan, and place in the refrigerator to chill.

When the mixture has set firmly, cut into $1/2$-inch cubes or diamond shapes, and serve with an equal amount of fresh and canned fruits. The nutty taste of almond gives an added dimension to a fruit salad. Alternatively, in China these almond cubes or diamonds are sometimes simply served on their own in sugary water or honeyed syrup.

## Hot Walnut 'Soup'
### (for 5–6 portions)

| | |
|---|---|
| 1 lb peeled walnuts | 5–6 tablespoons sugar |
| 4–5 tablespoons rice flour | 1 small can evaporated milk |
| $1^1/_2$ pints water | |

Mill the walnuts into a fine powder in a blender or liquidizer. Add the powdered walnut and rice flour to the water in a saucepan. Bring to the boil and simmer on a very gentle heat for 15 minutes, stirring continuously. Add the sugar and evaporated milk. Stir until the mixture reboils.

Serve hot in individual bowls.

## Fried Lotus Flower
### (for 4–6 portions)

| | |
|---|---|
| 12 pieces lotus petal | 4 egg whites |
| 4–5 tablespoons sweet bean paste | 2–3 tablespoons rainbow sugar |
| 2 tablespoons plain flour | oil for deep-frying |

Clean and dry the petals and halve each one. Spread some bean paste on one of the half petals and make a 'sandwich' with the other half. Use up all the petals in this way.

Beat the egg whites and flour in a basin until well blended. Dip the 'sandwiches' in the egg/flour mixture, and place 4 at a time in a wire basket to deep-fry for 2 minutes.

Arrange the lotus petal 'sandwiches' on a well-heated serving dish, sprinkle with rainbow sugar and serve.

### Glazed Chestnuts
(for 4–6 portions)

| | |
|---|---|
| 1 lb peeled chestnuts | 1$^1/_2$ breakfast cups sugar |
| 2$^1/_2$ breakfast cups water | $^1/_2$ cup honey |

Dissolve the sugar and honey in the water in a heavy saucepan, on a very low heat. When all the sugar has dissolved and the liquid becomes syrup-like, add the chestnuts. Cook for $^3/_4$–1 hour on a very gentle heat, turning the chestnuts over frequently to prevent sticking.

Place the chestnuts – separating them from one another – on a well-greased plate. Serve when cool.

Other types of nuts, such as walnuts, lotus seeds, etc., can all be treated in the same way.

### Glazed Potato Chips (or Apples)
(for 4–6 portions)

The Peking Brittle-glazed Apple is becoming a fairly well-known sweet in Peking restaurants in the West, but potatoes can be treated in the same manner with surprising results.

| | |
|---|---|
| 1 lb potatoes (or apples) | 3 tablespoons water |
| 6 heaped tablespoons sugar | oil for deep-frying |
| 2 tablespoons honey | 1 large glass bowl iced water |
| 2 tablespoons vegetable oil | |

Cut the potatoes into medium-sized chips. Place them in a wire basket, deep-fry them in three lots for 3 minutes each, and drain.

Gently heat the sugar, honey, oil and water in a pan. Stir until all the sugar has dissolved, stirring all the time. Continue to heat gently for another 2 minutes. Add the potato chips, turning them in the syrup until every piece is well covered.

Separate the chips from one another. As soon as they are detached drop them individually into the iced water. The sudden impact of coolness causes the film of 'syrup' over each chip to form into a sweet, brittle coating. After immersion, they should be retrieved immediately to prevent them from becoming sodden in the water and eaten at once. The sensation of teeth crackling through the thin sweet covering is one of the pleasures of this dish!

(For more conventional palates, exactly the same process can be followed with apples.)

### Water Chestnut 'Cake' (or Jelly)
(for 4–6 portions)

3–4 pieces fresh or canned water chestnut

$^1/_2$ tablespoon water chestnut flour

6 tablespoons sugar

1 pint water

2 packets gelatine

Slice the water chestnuts into thin matchstick strips. Blend the water chestnut flour with the sugar and water in a saucepan. Bring to the boil and simmer at a low heat. Add the gelatine and stir for 1 minute.

Pour the mixture into a well-greased, deep-sided flat dish. Sprinkle the water chestnut strips evenly over the mixture, and allow them to sink into the liquid. When cool, place the dish in a refrigerator for 2–3 hours, by which time the liquid should have set.

Turn the jelly on to a dish and cut evenly into 6 pieces. Serve each piece with some cream. The contrast between the texture of the fresh shredded water chestnut with the water chestnut jelly is stimulating to the palate.

## *Chilled Pears in Honey Syrup*
(for 6 portions)

6 pears (must be firm)
1$\frac{1}{2}$ cupfuls sugar
3 tablespoons honey

1–2 tablespoons sweet
liqueur or Crème de
Menthe

Peel the six pears, leaving the stalk for easy handling. Place them in a flat-bottomed pan and barely cover them with water. Bring to the boil and simmer for 20 minutes. Pour away half of the water and sprinkle the sugar over the pears. Simmer for another 20 minutes.

Arrange the pears on a flat deep-sided dish. Spoon half the syrupy juice over the pears. Place the dish in a refrigerator to chill for 2 hours.

Add the honey and sweet liqueur to the remainder of the syrupy juice and stir until well blended. Cool in the refrigerator, and when ready to serve pour the honey-wine syrup over each of the pears.

## *Eight Precious Pudding*
(for 8–12 portions)

Finally, a kind of Chinese Christmas pudding made with rice!

1 lb pudding rice
6 tablespoons sugar
4 tablespoons butter (or margarine)
1 cup sweet bean paste
$\frac{1}{2}$ cup lotus nuts
$\frac{1}{2}$ cup walnuts

$\frac{1}{4}$ cup dates
$\frac{1}{4}$ cup glacé cherries
$\frac{1}{4}$ cup green candied fruits
$\frac{1}{4}$ cup orange or red candied peel
$\frac{1}{4}$ cup dried dragon eyes (Loon Ngaan)

Blanch the nuts. Add 1 pint of water, sugar and a quarter of the butter to the rice. Bring to the boil and heat very gently, until the rice is almost completely dry. Chop the dates and candied fruits into halves or quarters.

Heavily grease the walls of a large mould or basin with the remainder of the margarine or butter, and cover with a thin ($^1/_4$-inch) layer of rice. Stud the rice with the dates, candied fruits and nuts, pushing them through the walls of the rice. Fill the basin with alternate layers of rice and sweet bean paste (each layer of rice being three or four times the thickness of the paste), studding each layer of rice with the remainder of the candied fruits, nuts, peels and dates, covering the top with a layer of rice.

Place the basin in a steamer and steam steadily for 60–70 minutes.

Turn the 'pudding' on to a dish, and serve as you would serve a Christmas pudding.

# Index